# Greater Milwaukee Outings on the Cheap (2017/2018)

Jill Florence Lackey & Rick Petrie

**MECAH Publishing**
Milwaukee Ethnic Collection of Arts and Humanities

Milwaukee Wisconsin
www.mecahmilwaukee.com

For more information on this book, or to order, visit www.mecahmilwaukee.com

ISBN-13: 978-1541236141
ISBN-10: 1541236149

# Table of Contents

**Year-round events**                                    **3**
    Milwaukee                          3
    Greater Milwaukee                  11

**Winter events**                                        **13**
    *National holiday-specific*        13
        December events     13
        New Year's          18
        Valentine's Day     18
        Dr. Martin Luther King Day    19
    *General*                          19
        Milwaukee           19
        Greater Milwaukee   25

**Spring events**                                        **28**
    *National holiday-specific*        28
        St. Patrick's Day   28
        Easter              28
        Memorial Day        29
    *General*                          30
        Milwaukee           30
        Greater Milwaukee   34

**Summer events**                                        **41**
    *National holiday-specific*        41
        Juneteenth Day      41
        Father's Day        41
        July 4              42
    *General*                          45
        Milwaukee           45
        Greater Milwaukee   61

**Fall events**                                          **77**
    *National holiday-specific*        77
        Labor Day           77
        Halloween           78
        Veterans' Day       80
        Thanksgiving        80
    *General*                          80
        Milwaukee           80
        Greater Milwaukee   89

**Index**                                                **94**

**How to use this book**: Events are *not* listed chronologically within the seasons. Milwaukee events are always listed first, followed by Greater Milwaukee events. Indexes are provided at the end and list outings by (1) towns/cities, (2) targeted participants, and (3) event categories. Readers may submit or correct events for the next book edition. Directions are on the last page.

# Year-round events (not in chronological order)

Listings do NOT include classes, workouts, or clubs

LISTINGS ONLY INCLUDE RECURRING EVENTS UNDER $10 PER ADULT ADMISSION. THE ADMISSION PRICE ONLY COVERS THE ENTRANCE FEES AND DOES NOT INCLUDE THE PRICE OF FOOD, RIDES, GOODS, RAFFLE TICKETS, OR OTHER ITEMS THAT MAY BE PART OF THE EVENT.

PLEASE ALWAYS CHECK THE CONTACT INFO FOR ANY RECENT CHANGES IN THESE EVENTS.

| OLD SOUTH SIDE SETTLEMENT MUSEUM (Yr1) | | | |
|---|---|---|---|
| **When?** | **Where?** | **Description and contact info** | **Admission** |
| By reservation, call 414 672-8090 | 707 W. Lincoln Ave. | Tour of museum replicates the early rooms of Polish, Kashubian, and Mexican settlers in neighborhood. http://socmilwaukee.org/index/programs/museum/ | $10 adult; $8 children, seniors |

| SELF-GUIDED TOUR OF FOREST HOME CEMETERY (Yr2) | | | |
|---|---|---|---|
| **When?** | **Where?** | **Description and contact info** | **Admission** |
| Daily 8am-4:30pm | 2405 W. Forest Home | Tour the beautiful Chapel Gardens, Landmark Chapel, and the Hall of History that tells the story of Milwaukee dignitaries, including European founders of Milwaukee, several mayors, major African American activists, and brewery tycoons. (414) 645-2632 | Free |

| MILLER-COORS TOUR (Yr3) | | | |
|---|---|---|---|
| **When?** | **Where?** | **Description and contact info** | **Admission** |
| Usually Mon.-Sat. every 30 min. between 10:30am and 3:30pm | 4251 W. State Street | Indoor/outdoor guided walking tour of Miller Valley, with over 155 years of brewing history. www.millercoors.com/Brewery-Tours/Milwaukee-Brewery-Tour/Tour-Information.aspx | Free |

| WALKER'S POINT CENTER FOR THE ARTS (Yr4) | | | |
|---|---|---|---|
| **When?** | **Where?** | **Description and contact info** | **Admission** |
| Tue.-Sat. 12-5pm | 839 S 5th St. | Ongoing exhibitions in a community setting. http://wpca-milwaukee.org/ | Free to look |

| DEAN JENSEN GALLERY (Yr5) | | | |
|---|---|---|---|
| **When?** | **Where?** | **Description and contact info** | **Admission** |
| Wed.-Fri. 10am-6pm; Sat. 10am-4pm | 759 N Water St, | Described in the national art press as ranking as one of Milwaukee's finest commercial art spaces. | Free to look |

| CHUDNOW MUSEUM OF YESTERYEAR (Yr6) | | | |
|---|---|---|---|
| **When?** | **Where?** | **Description and contact info** | **Admission** |
| Wed.-Sat. 10am-4pm, Sun. 12-4pm | 839 N. 11th St. | Museum that features rooms, history, and artifacts collected between WWI and WWII. http://chudnowmuseum.org/index.html | $5, $4 kids 7-17, college students with ID, seniors |

| LOW COST MOVIES: DOWNER THEATER (Yr7) | | | |
|---|---|---|---|
| **When?** | **Where?** | **Description and contact info** | **Admission** |
| Sat., Sun. early show | 2589 N. Downer Ave. | A Landmark arthouse theater. https://www.landmarktheatres.com/milwaukee | $7.50 |

| LOW COST MOVIES: ORIENTAL THEATER (Yr8) | | | |
|---|---|---|---|
| **When?** | **Where?** | **Description and contact info** | **Admission** |
| Sat., Sun. early show | 2230 N. Farwell Ave. | A Landmark arthouse theater. https://www.landmarktheatres.com/milwaukee | $7.50 |

| KERR GALLERY (Yr9) | | | |
|---|---|---|---|
| **When?** | **Where?** | **Description and contact info** | **Admission** |
| Daily 10am-5pm | The collection can be viewed in downtown Milwaukee at the Riverview Antique Market, 175 S. Water St. | Features art that is tribal or folk in origin. http://www.thekerrgallery.com/ | Free to look |

| VILLA TERRACE DECORATIVE ARTS MUSEUM (Yr10) | | | |
|---|---|---|---|
| **When?** | **Where?** | **Description and contact info** | **Admission** |
| Wed. thru Sun. 1-5pm | 2220 N. Terrace Ave. | Self-guided tour of mansion informed by the design of a villa in Lombardy, Italy, complete with Renaissance Garden, and antique furnishings and artifacts. http://www.villaterracemuseum.org/tours.html | $7, $5 seniors, military & students |

| ORANGE GALLERY (Yr11) | | | |
|---|---|---|---|
| **When?** | **Where?** | **Description and contact info** | **Admission** |
| Fri., Sat., Sun., 12-6pm | 1438 E Russell Ave, | Consignment shop to showcase the best in local (and some not local) artists. http://orangegallerymke.com/ | Free to look |

| CHARLES ALLIS ART MUSEUM (Yr12) | | | |
|---|---|---|---|
| **When?** | **Where?** | **Description and contact info** | **Admission** |
| Wed. thru Sun. 1-5pm | 1801 N. Prospect Ave. | Self-guided tour of Tudor-style mansion of entrepreneur Charles Allis designed by Milwaukee architect Alexander Eschweiler in early 20th century. http://www.charlesallis.org/ | $7, $5 seniors & students |

| MILWAUKEE COUNTY HISTORICAL SOCIETY (Yr13) | | | |
|---|---|---|---|
| **When?** | **Where?** | **Description and contact info** | **Admission** |
| Mon. thru Sat., 9:30am-5pm | 910 N. Old World Third St. | Permanent and rotating exhibits of Milwaukee County's history plus a research library. http://www.milwaukeehistory.net/ | $7 for special exhibits; kids <12 free |

| MOVIE TIME AT THE CHARLES ALLIS MUSEUM (Yr14) | | | |
|---|---|---|---|
| When? | Where? | Description and contact info | Admission |
| Select Weds. 7:30pm | 1801 N. Prospect Ave. | Classic films from the 30s and 40s from rare collection of Milwaukee film historian Dale Kuntz. http://www.charlesallis.org/movietime.html | $7, $5 seniors & students |

| MONTHLY FAMILY MAGIC SHOW (Yr15) | | | |
|---|---|---|---|
| When? | Where? | Description and contact info | Admission |
| 1ST Sat. every month, 11-11:30 am | Best Western, 5105 S. Howell Ave. | An interactive show that combines comedy, mental magic, and audience participation. http://www.twobrothersonemind.com/ | $5 |

| HAGGERTY MUSEUM OF ART (Yr16) | | | |
|---|---|---|---|
| When? | Where? | Description and contact info | Admission |
| Mon., Tue., Wed., Fri. 10am-4:30pm, Thu. 10am-8pm; Sun, 12-5pm | Marquette campus at corner of 13th & Clybourn Sts. | Permanent collections include Old Masters' prints, Ralph Steiner photos, Marc Chagall Bible series, Barbara Morgan photos, and Finnegan, Fishman, Tatalovich, and Rojtman collections. http://www.marquette.edu/haggerty/ | Free |

| TOUR OF BEULAH BRINTON HOUSE (Yr17) | | | |
|---|---|---|---|
| When? | Where? | Description and contact info | Admission |
| Every third Sat. of the month, 1-4pm | 2590 S. Superior St. | Tour the home of a woman most responsible for acclimating new immigrants to the town of Bay View in the late 19th century. www.bayviewhistoricalsociety.org/ | Free |

| SELF-GUIDED TOUR OF VA GROUNDS (Yr18) | | | |
|---|---|---|---|
| When? | Where? | Description and contact info | Admission |
| Daily, daylight | Just north of Zablocki VA Medical Center, 5000 W. National Ave. | A walk through the historic district just north of the Zablocki VA Medical Center, which includes the Soldiers' Home, barracks building, old fire station, old hospital, Ward Memorial Theater, and more. http://www.milwaukee.va.gov/visitors/campus.asp | Free |

| MOVIES AT SOUTHGATE CINEMA (Yr19) | | | |
|---|---|---|---|
| When? | Where? | Description and contact info | Admission |
| Daily (see website for hours) | 3320 S. 30th St. | Popular movies at a Marcus Theater. http://www.marcustheatres.com/theatre-locations/southgate-cinema-milwaukee | $10, $7.50 kids, military (with ID), seniors; less for matinees |

| WEEKLY WALKS IN LINDSAY HEIGHTS (Yr20) | | | |
|---|---|---|---|
| When? | Where? | Description and contact info | Admission |
| Wed.'s starts 6pm | 11th and Lloyd Sts. | Opportunity to learn more about neighborhood, meet neighbors, talk to alderman. https://www.facebook.com/Lindsay-Heights-CPC-MKE-132770993733206/ | Free |

## JEWISH MUSEUM OF MILWAUKEE (Yr21)

| When? | Where? | Description and contact info | Admission |
|---|---|---|---|
| Mon.-Thu 10am-4pm; Fri. 10am-2pm, Sun. 12-4pm | 1360 N. Prospect Ave. | Visit museum dedicated to preserving and presenting the history of the Jewish people in southeastern Wisconsin and celebrating the continuum of Jewish heritage and culture. http://jewishmuseummilwaukee.org/about/ | $6 adults, $5 seniors, $15 families, free kids <6 |

## GROHMANN MUSEUM (Yr22)

| When? | Where? | Description and contact info | Admission |
|---|---|---|---|
| Mon.-Fri. 9am-5pm, Sat. 12-6pm, Sun. 1-4pm | 1000 N. Broadway | More than 1,000 paintings and sculptures representing the evolution of human work. http://www.msoe.edu/about-msoe/grohmann-museum/ | $5; $3 seniors, students, free kids <12 |

## ART BAR (Yr23)

| When? | Where? | Description and contact info | Admission |
|---|---|---|---|
| Daily 3pm-12am | 722 E. Burleigh St. | Permanent and temporary art exhibits. https://www.facebook.com/artbarmke/ | Adults free |

## THE GREEN GALLERY (Yr24)

| When? | Where? | Description and contact info | Admission |
|---|---|---|---|
| Wed.-Sat. 2-6pm | 1500 N. Farwell Ave. | Permanent and temporary art exhibits. http://www.thegreengallery.biz/gallery-info | Free to look |

## ART 'N ODDITIES (Yr25)

| When? | Where? | Description and contact info | Admission |
|---|---|---|---|
| Mon., Tues. 10am-3pm; Wed., Thu., Fri. 10am-4:30pm; Sat. 10am-2pm. | 5833 W Lincoln Ave. | A unique gallery of art and artists from around the world with a flair. http://www.artnoddities.com/Art_N_Oddities/Home.html | Free to look |

## KATIE GINGRASS GALLERY (Yr26)

| When? | Where? | Description and contact info | Admission |
|---|---|---|---|
| Tue.-Sat. 10am-5pm | 241 N. Broadway | Contemporary gallery of art and fine crafts with exhibitions of recognized artists. http://www.gingrassgallery.com/ | Free to look |

## OPEN SWIM—PULASKI (Yr27)

| When? | Where? | Description and contact info | Admission |
|---|---|---|---|
| Daily, 1-5pm, holiday times vary | Pulaski Park, 2701 S. 16th St. | Open swim year-round at indoor pool with diving boards, locker rooms, vending machines. http://county.milwaukee.gov/IndoorPools9146/PulaskiPool.htm | $4, $3 kids <12 |

## OASIS CENTER FOR OLDER ADULTS (Yr27a)

| When? | Where? | Description and contact info | Admission |
|---|---|---|---|
| See website | 2414 W. Mitchell St. | Wide variety of programs for active older adults. http://wwww.MilwaukeeRecreation.net | $10 residents |

| OPEN SWIM—NOYES (Yr28) | | | |
|---|---|---|---|
| When? | Where? | Description and contact info | Admission |
| Daily, 1-5pm, holiday times vary | Noyes Park, 8235 W. Good Hope Rd. | Open swim year-round at indoor pool with diving boards, locker rooms, vending machines. http://county.milwaukee.gov/IndoorPools9146.htm | $4, $3 kids <12 |

| ARCHAEOLOGY LECTURES (Yr29) | | | |
|---|---|---|---|
| When? | Where? | Description and contact info | Admission |
| Various times, fall and spring semesters, Sat. or Sun., see website | Sabin Hall, 3415 N. Downer Ave. | Lectures by renowned archaeologists for an educated lay audience, sponsored by the Archaeological Institute of America—Milwaukee Society. http://www4.uwm.edu/archlab/AIA/lectures.cfm | Free |

| MILWAUKEE ASIAN MARKET (Yr30) | | | |
|---|---|---|---|
| When? | Where? | Description and contact info | Admission |
| Daily, 7am-7pm | 6300 N. 76th Street | Hundreds of stalls of Asian food, clothing, toiletries, cosmetics, and other goods. (414) 760-3771 | Free |

| HANK AARON TRAIL (Yr31) | | | |
|---|---|---|---|
| When? | Where? | Description and contact info | Admission |
| Daily | Multiple access points; see map on website | Opportunity to enjoy natural and urban views and walk or bike trail across Milwaukee, from the lakefront to 94th Place. http://hankaaronstatetrail.org/ | Free |

| NORTHPOINT LIGHTHOUSE MUSEUM (Yr32) | | | |
|---|---|---|---|
| When? | Where? | Description and contact info | Admission |
| Sat. & Sun. 1-4pm | Northpoint Lighthouse, 2650 N. Wahl Ave. | A historic, maritime experience, with artifacts related to the history of the Great Lakes. http://northpointlighthouse.org/ | $8, $5 seniors & kids 5-11, free kids<4 |

| GALLERY AT MILWAUKEE INSTITUTE OF ART & DESIGN (Yr33) | | | |
|---|---|---|---|
| When? | Where? | Description and contact info | Admission |
| Mon.-Sat. 10am-5pm | 273 E. Erie St. | Rotating exhibitions of renowned artists, MIAD students, and MIAD faculty. http://www.miad.edu/ | Free |

| ECO ART WEDNESDAYS (Yr34) | | | |
|---|---|---|---|
| When? | Where? | Description and contact info | Admission |
| Weds., 4-5:30pm | Menomonee Valley 3700 W. Pierce | Children work on nature-inspired recycled arts and crafts. Take home own creation every week! Register at http://urbanecologycenter.org/programs-events-main.html | $5 per child |

| EARLY MORNING BIRDWALK (Yr35) | | | |
|---|---|---|---|
| **When?** | **Where?** | **Description and contact info** | **Admission** |
| Most Tue.'s. 8-10am | Menomonee Valley, 3700 W. Pierce St. | A walk for bird watchers of all ability levels to explore Three Bridges Park for birds. http://urbanecologycenter.org/programs-events-main.html | Free, but might need to register |

| TOUR OF MUSEUM OF WISCONSIN EVANGELICAL LUTHERAN SYNOD (WELS) (Yr36) | | | |
|---|---|---|---|
| **When?** | **Where?** | **Description and contact info** | **Admission** |
| By appointment | Salem Lutheran Landmark Church, lower level, 6814 N. 107th St. | Tour of more than 1,000 artifacts and pictures of the Wisconsin Evangelical Lutheran Synod. Email Joel.Pless@wlc.edu | Free, but donations welcome |

| EARLY MORNING BIRDWALK--WASHINGTON (Yr37) | | | |
|---|---|---|---|
| **When?** | **Where?** | **Description and contact info** | **Admission** |
| Most Wed.'s 8-10am | Washington Park, 1859 N. 40th St. | A walk for bird watchers of all ability levels to explore Washington Park for birds. http://urbanecologycenter.org/programs-events-main.html | Free, but might need to register |

| EARLY MORNING BIRDWALK--RIVERSIDE (Yr38) | | | |
|---|---|---|---|
| **When?** | **Where?** | **Description and contact info** | **Admission** |
| Most Thu.'s 8-10:30am | Riverside Park 1500 E. Park Pl. | A walk for bird watchers of all ability levels to explore Riverside Park for birds. http://urbanecologycenter.org/programs-events-main.html | Free, but might need to register |

| UNGUIDED TOUR OF BASILICA OF ST. JOSAPHAT (Yr39) | | | |
|---|---|---|---|
| **When?** | **Where?** | **Description and contact info** | **Admission** |
| Mon., 9am-4pm | Visitor's Center, Basilica of St. Josaphat, 2333 S. 6th St. | Opportunity to see and learn about one of the most beautiful churches in America with informational exhibits on lower level. http://thebasilica.org/ | Free |

| GUIDED TOUR OF BASILICA OF ST. JOSAPHAT (Yr40) | | | |
|---|---|---|---|
| **When?** | **Where?** | **Description and contact info** | **Admission** |
| Sun.'s, after 10am mass | Basilica of St. Josaphat, 2333 S. 6th St. | Opportunity to see and learn about one of the most beautiful churches in America. http://thebasilica.org/visit | Free |

| UWM SCIENCE BAG (Yr41) | | | |
|---|---|---|---|
| **When?** | **Where?** | **Description and contact info** | **Admission** |
| Fall and spring semesters, Fri. 8pm (occasional Sun. matinee) | Physics Building, at E. Kenwood Blvd. and N. Cramer St., rm. 137 | One-hour shows designed to educate and entertain all age groups on various aspects of science, supported by College of Letters & Science. http://www4.uwm.edu/letsci/sciencebag/ | Free |

| MILWAUKEE ART MUSEUM (Yr42) | | | |
|---|---|---|---|
| When? | Where? | Description and contact info | Admission |
| 1ST Thu. of each month | 700 N. Art Museum Dr. | An architectural landmark with world-class exhibits. http://mam.org/ | Free (on date designated) |

| BETTY BRINN CHILDREN'S MUSEUM (Yr43) | | | |
|---|---|---|---|
| When? | Where? | Description and contact info | Admission |
| 3rd Thu. of each month | 929 E. Wisconsin Ave. | Hands-on displays that teach science, business, and art, field trips and educational programs, parties, and a toddler section. www.bbcmkids.org/calendar/ | Free (on date designated) |

| MITCHELL PARK DOMES (Yr44) | | | |
|---|---|---|---|
| When? | Where? | Description and contact info | Admission |
| Mon. 9am-12pm | 524 S. Layton Blvd. | A place to experience a desert oasis, a tropical jungle, and special floral gardens all in one morning. http://county.milwaukee.gov/MitchellParkConserva10116.htm | Free (on date designated) |

| MILWAUKEE PUBLIC MUSEUM (Yr45) | | | |
|---|---|---|---|
| When? | Where? | Description and contact info | Admission |
| 1ST Thu. each month | 800 W. Wells St. | Chance to visit one of the premier natural history and science facilities, world- renowned for its exhibits, collections, ongoing scientific research and educational exhibits. www.mpm.edu/ | Free (on date designated) |

| MORNING GLORY GALLERY (Yr46) | | | |
|---|---|---|---|
| When? | Where? | Description and contact info | Admission |
| Thu., Fri., Sat. 12-6pm | 929 N Water St, | Fine crafts from Wisconsin artists—ceramics, fiber, glass, jewelry and more.. http://www.mggallery.org/ | Free to look |

| LITTLE NATURE MUSEUM (Yr47) | | | |
|---|---|---|---|
| When? | Where? | Description and contact info | Admission |
| Mon.-Fri., 4-5pm, Sat., Sun. 3-4pm | Hawthorn Glen, 1130 N. 60th St. | Native animals of Wisconsin, including tree frogs, turtles, crow, 6-foot bullsnake. 475-5300 | Free |

| FREE FAMILY SWIM—WASHINGTON HS (Yr48) | | | |
|---|---|---|---|
| When? | Where? | Description and contact info | Admission |
| Tue.'s 6:00-6:55pm females; 7:00-7:55pm males | Washington H.S., 2525 N. Sherman Blvd., enter main gym door on Sherman Blvd. | Indoor swimming with swim caps available for purchase (children 7 and under must be accompanied by adult). 875-6025 | Free |

| FREE FAMILY SWIM—GAENSLEN HS (Yr49) | | | |
|---|---|---|---|
| When? | Where? | Description and contact info | Admission |
| Wed.'s 6:50-7:50pm | Gaenslen Elementary, 1250 E. Burleigh St., north door #4 | Indoor swimming with swim caps available for purchase (children 7 and under must be accompanied by adult). 267-5734. | Free |

| MERRILL PARK PLAYFIELD/COMMUNITY CENTER (Yr50) | | | |
|---|---|---|---|
| **When?** | **Where?** | **Description and contact info** | **Admission** |
| Daily 10am-7pm | 461 N. 35th St. | Arts and crafts, computer lab, board games, video games, movie night and foose ball. http://www.neighborhoodlink.com/Merrill_Park/pages/223713 | Free |

| FREE FAMILY SWIM—NORTH DIVISION (Yr51) | | | |
|---|---|---|---|
| **When?** | **Where?** | **Description and contact info** | **Admission** |
| Wed.'s 7:05-8:15pm | North Division H.S., 1011 W. Center St., enter west side of bldg. | Indoor swimming with swim caps available for purchase (children 7 and under must be accompanied by adult). .(414) 267-5077. | Free |

| FREE FAMILY SWIM—SOUTH DIVISION (Yr52) | | | |
|---|---|---|---|
| **When?** | **Where?** | **Description and contact info** | **Admission** |
| Mon.'s & Wed.'s 7:30-8:40pm | South Division H.S., 1615 W. Lapham Blvd., enter east door. | Indoor swimming with swim caps available for purchase (children 7 and under must be accompanied by adult). 902-8377. | Free |

| FREE FAMILY SWIM—MORSE-MARSHALL (Yr53) | | | |
|---|---|---|---|
| **When?** | **Where?** | **Description and contact info** | **Admission** |
| Wed.'s, 7:30-8:40pm | Morse-Marshall H.S., 4141 N. 64th St., enter door #10 | Indoor swimming with swim caps available for purchase (children 7 and under must be accompanied by adult). 393-2502 | Free |

| FREE FAMILY SWIM—RIVERSIDE (Yr54) | | | |
|---|---|---|---|
| **When?** | **Where?** | **Description and contact info** | **Admission** |
| Late Jun.-early Aug., Tue.'s & Thu.'s 1:05-2:15pm | Riverside H.S., 1615 E. Locust St., enter door #5; 906-4959 | Indoor swimming with swim caps available for purchase (children 7 and under must be accompanied by adult). 393-2502 | Free |

| BASKETBALL—BAY VIEW (Yr55) | | | |
|---|---|---|---|
| **When?** | **Where?** | **Description and contact info** | **Admission** |
| Wed. 1-3pm | Beulah Brinton Community Center, 2555 S. Bay St. | Basketball in community center. (414) 481-2494 | Free |

| BILLIARDS—BAY VIEW (Yr56) | | | |
|---|---|---|---|
| **When?** | **Where?** | **Description and contact info** | **Admission** |
| Mon.-Fri. 8:30am-3pm | Beulah Brinton Community Center, 2555 S. Bay St. | Billiards in community center. (414) 481-2494 | Free |

| CARD PLAYING—BAY VIEW (Yr 57) | | | |
|---|---|---|---|
| **When?** | **Where?** | **Description and contact info** | **Admission** |
| Mon.-Fri. 8:30am-3pm | Beulah Brinton Community Center, 2555 S. Bay St. | Organized card playing in community center. (414) 481-2494 | Free |

| FRENCH FILM SERIES (Yr58) | | | |
|---|---|---|---|
| When? | Where? | Description and contact info | Admission |
| 3rd Sat. of every month, 1pm | Alliance Francaise, 1800 E. Capital Dr. | New and classic films by new and acclaimed directors. http://www.afmilwaukee.org/share-enjoy/special-events | Free |

| WALK THROUGH MILWAUKEE'S LATINO HISTORY (Yr59) | | | |
|---|---|---|---|
| When | Where? | Description and contact info | Admission |
| Daily, 10-4pm | United Community Center, 1028 S. 9th St. | Opportunity to learn about Latino history by visiting tannery and foundry exhibits, photos, and art inside the UCC building, and historical murals on two sides of Bruce Guadalupe School next door. http://www.unitedcc.org/index.htm | Free |

| MILWAUKEE FIRE MUSEUM (Yr60) | | | |
|---|---|---|---|
| When? | Where? | Description and contact info | Admission |
| 1st Sun. of each month, 1-4pm, (except holidays) | 1516 W. Oklahoma Ave. | Opportunity to see exhibits and artifacts of the Milwaukee Fire Department back to the 1800s; stories of history of Department and fires. http://city.milwaukee.gov/MUSEUMHISTORICALSOCIETY.htm#.VkOAEMArLIU | Free |

| DAVID BARNETT ART GALLERY (Yr61) | | | |
|---|---|---|---|
| When? | Where? | Description and contact info | Admission |
| Tues.-Sat. 11am-5pm | 1024 E. State St. | Chance to visit gallery that specializes in European and American masters, regional and nationally recognized artists, and "emerging" Wisconsin artists. www.davidbarnettgallery.com/Asset.asp?AssetID=60682&AKey=2PRXC5PX | Free |

| WALK THROUGH OLD BRONZEVILLE (Yr62) | | | |
|---|---|---|---|
| When? | Where? | Description and contact info | Admission |
| Daily, by appt., 1:30-4 | Lapham Park Apartments and Senior Center 1901 N. 6th St. | Opportunity to learn about old Bronzeville by visiting replica of the once thriving Walnut Street, the heart of Bronzeville, in lower level of Lapham Center. To reserve time, call (414) 286-8859 | Free |

- - - - - - - - - - - - - - - - - - - - - - - - - - - - - - - - - - - - - - - - - - - - - - - - - - -

| GALLERY 505—WHITEFISH BAY (Yr63) | | | |
|---|---|---|---|
| When? | Where? | Description and contact info | Admission |
| Mon.-Fri. 10am-8pm; Sat., 10am-5pm; Sun. 12-4pm | 505 E. Silver Spring Dr., Whitefish Bay | Oil and acrylic paintings from around the world. http://www.gallery-505.com/ | Free to look |

### KILBOURNTOWN HOUSE—SHOREWOOD (Yr64)

| When? | Where? | Description and contact info | Admission |
|---|---|---|---|
| Sat.'s. 10-4pm; Sun.'s 12-4pm, by appointment | Estabrook Park on Estabrook Dr. just north of Capitol Dr., Shorewood | Greek Revival house built in 1844 by Benjamin Church, a carpenter from New York which was originally located in the section of Milwaukee known as Kilbourntown. Call 414-273-8288 for appointment. http://www.milwaukeehistory.net/historic-sites-2/kilbourntown-house/ | $2 |

### LOWELL DAMON HOUSE—WAUWATOSA (Yr65)

| When? | Where? | Description and contact info | Admission |
|---|---|---|---|
| Suns. 1-5pm (no holidays); by appointment | 2107 Wauwatosa Ave. (76th St.) Wauwatosa | House that is believed to be Wauwatosa's oldest residence and stands as a classic example of a colonial home. Call 414-273-8288 for appointment. http://www.milwaukeehistory.net/historic-sites-2/lowell-damon-house/ | $2 |

### JEREMIAH CURTIN HOUSE—GREENDALE (Yr66)

| When? | Where? | Description and contact info | Admission |
|---|---|---|---|
| May 15-Oct. 15, by appointment only | W. Grange Ave. and S. 84th St., Greendale | Home of Irish immigrants who settled in the old Town of Greenfield in the mid-1830s. Call 414-273-8288 for appointment. http://www.milwaukeehistory.net/historic-sites-2/jeremiah-curtin-house/ | $2 |

### BINGO AT THE POLISH CENTER OF WISCONSIN-FRANKLIN (Yr67)

| When? | Where? | Description and contact info | Admission |
|---|---|---|---|
| Wed.'s 6 and 7:30 pm | 6941 S. 68th St., Franklin | Weekly and multi-generational bingo in beautiful, naturally-lit building. www.polishcenterofwisconsin.org | Soft cards: 3-on for $5.00; 6-on for $10.00 |

### LOW COST MOVIES: VALUE CINEMA-OAK CREEK (Yr68)

| When? | Where? | Description and contact info | Admission |
|---|---|---|---|
| Daily, matinees and evenings | 6912 S. 27th St., Oak Creek | A Marcus Theater with 8 screens and value pricing, https://marcustheatres.com/theatre-locations/value-cinema-oak-creek | $2 Wed.-Mon., $1 Tue. |

### LOW COST MOVIES: RIDGE THEATER-NEW BERLIN (Yr69)

| When? | Where? | Description and contact info | Admission |
|---|---|---|---|
| Wed., Fri. before 5:30 | 5200 S. Moorland Rd., New Berlin | A Marcus Theater with 19 auditoriums, food, and value prices. http://www.marcustheatres.com/theatre-locations/ridge-cinema-new-berlin | $8.50 matinee, $5 seniors, students ($7 for 3D) |

# Winter: December, January, February (not in chronological order)

## National Holiday-Specific

## December holidays

| COCOA WITH THE CLAUSES (Wi 1) | | | |
|---|---|---|---|
| When? | Where? | Description and contact info | Admission |
| Early Dec., Sat. 11am-2pm | Cathedral Square Park, 520 E. Wells St. | Chance to take pictures of your kids with holiday characters, listen to Christmas music, and share your wish list with Santa. www.milwaukeedowntown.com/about-us/special-events/milwaukee-holiday-lights-festival/cocoa-with-the-clauses | Free |

| CHRISTMAS PARADE (Wi 2) | | | |
|---|---|---|---|
| When? | Where? | Description and contact info | Admission |
| Mid to late Nov., Sat. 9:30am | Route begins at Astor & Kilbourn and travels west on Kilbourn to Old World Third | Parade with marching bands, balloons, floats, celebrities, animals, and Santa. http://www.milwaukeeparade.com/ | Free |

| BREAKFAST WITH SANTA (Wi 3) | | | |
|---|---|---|---|
| When? | Where? | Description and contact info | Admission |
| Mid Dec., Sat. 9:30am-12pm | Kosciuszko Community Center, 2201 S. 7th St. | All-you-can-eat breakfast of pancakes, sausage, beverage, with Santa, and photos of Santa (first 250 receive gift bag). http://county.milwaukee.gov/BreakfastwithSanta16429.htm | $3 |

| SANTA HUSTLE 5K MILWAUKEE WALK/RUN (Wi 4) | | | |
|---|---|---|---|
| When? | Where? | Description and contact info | Admission |
| Early Dec., Sat., begins 8:30am | Veteran's Park, 1010 N. Lincoln Memorial Dr. | One of the largest, growing races as thousands of Santas hit the streets with candy, cookies, and festive music along the way. http://www.santahustle.com/milwaukee/event-info/ | Free to watch |

## SALVATION ARMY ANNUAL CHRISTMAS FEAST (Wi 5)

| When? | Where? | Description and contact info | Admission |
|---|---|---|---|
| Christmas Day, 11am-2:30pm | Wisconsin Center, 400 W. Wisconsin Ave. | Annual Christmas feast for every member of the community to partake, with Santa. http://www.wisconsincenter.org/events/the-salvation-armys-christmas-family-feast/ | Free, but donation always welcome |

## KWANZAA AT BODY & SOUL (Wi 6)

| When? | Where? | Description and contact info | Admission |
|---|---|---|---|
| Late Dec., see hours on website | Body and Soul Healing Arts Center, 3617 N. 48th St. | Opportunity to experience fun and education that will be taking place at Body and Soul during three of the seven days of Kwanzaa https://www.evensi.us/kwanzaa-at-body-and-soul-the-body-soul-healing-arts-center/191485022 | Free |

## KWANZAA—BHM (Wi 7)

| When? | Where? | Description and contact info | Admission |
|---|---|---|---|
| Late Dec., see website | Wisconsin Black Historical Center, 2620 W. Center St. | An African-American cultural festival.. www.wbhsm.org/Home.htm | Free |

## WINTER WONDERLANDS CELEBRATION (Wi 7a)

| When? | Where? | Description and contact info | Admission |
|---|---|---|---|
| Late Dec., see website | Journey House, 2110 W. Scott St., | Opportunity to meet Santa and Mrs. Claus, do crafts, eat cookies and refreshments, and receive clothing. www.journeyhouse.org | Free (families) |

## JINGLE BUS RIDES (Wi 8)

| When? | Where? | Description and contact info | Admission |
|---|---|---|---|
| Late Nov., Fri, Sat, Sun. 6-8:20pm | The Shops of Grand Avenue - Center Court, 275 W. Wisconsin Ave. | 40-minute tour of festive downtown Milwaukee featuring key attractions and landmarks. http://www.milwaukeedowntown.com/milwaukee-events/jingle-bus-rides/ | $1 |

## FESTIVUS ON BRADY (Wi 9)

| When? | Where? | Description and contact info | Admission |
|---|---|---|---|
| Early Dec., Sat. 9:30pm-1:30am. | Brady Street | Opportunity to air grievances and participate in feats of strength to win Festivus pole, per Festivus Seinfeld episode in 1997. http://bradystreet.org/documents/28-festivus- | Free |

## TREE LIGHTING IN THE WARD (Wi 10)

| When? | Where? | Description and contact info | Admission |
|---|---|---|---|
| Early Dec. Fri. eve | Chicago & Broadway in Third Ward | Bands, tree lighting, bake sales, carriage rides, dancers. www.historicthirdward.org/events/christmas.php | Free |

## HOLIDAY PAGEANT (Wi 11)

| When? | Where? | Description and contact info | Admission |
|---|---|---|---|
| Mid Dec., Fri. 5:30-7pm | Neighborhood House, 2819 W. Richardson Pl. | Art activities, games, vendors, kids' performances, lite dinner, and more. Register with Tasha at (414) 933-6161 x142 www.neighborhoodhousemke.org | Free |

| MILWAUKEE HOLIDAY LIGHTS (Wi 12) | | | |
|---|---|---|---|
| When? | Where? | Description and contact info | Admission |
| Mid Nov. – late Dec., weekdays, 5-10pm | Cathedral Square, Pere Marquette Park, and Zeidler Union Square | Six-week festival to spread holiday spirit with animated light displays in the parks and hundreds of events. http://county.milwaukee.gov/ParksCalendar | Free |

| NOT A CREATURE WAS STIRRING—HOLIDAY FLORAL SHOW (Wi 13) | | | |
|---|---|---|---|
| When? | Where? | Description and contact info | Admission |
| Dec., Mon.-Fri. 9am-5pm; Sat., Sun. holidays 9am-4pm | Mitchell Park Domes, 524 S. Layton Blvd. | Holiday floral show at the Horticultural Center. http://county.milwaukee.gov/ParksCalendar | $7, $5 students, disabled, youth 6-18; free 6 |

| CRAFT & BAKE SALE (Wi 14) | | | |
|---|---|---|---|
| When? | Where? | Description and contact info | Admission |
| Mid Dec., Sun. after all masses | Basilica of St. Josaphat, | Opportunity to purchase crafts or baked goods for holiday gifts. http://thebasilica.org/events | Free |

| ANNUAL CHRISTMAS IN THE WARD (Wi 15) | | | |
|---|---|---|---|
| When? | Where? | Description and contact info | Admission |
| Early Dec., Fri. 5-8pm, Sat. 10am-6pm | Along streets of the Third Ward | Chance to experience an old-fashioned tree lighting ceremony, fireworks, horse-drawn carriage rides, Santa, live reindeer and other outdoor holiday entertainment. http://www.historicthirdward.org/events/christmas.php | Free |

| HOLIDAY CELEBRATION AND TREE LIGHTING (Wi 16) | | | |
|---|---|---|---|
| When? | Where? | Description and contact info | Admission |
| Early Dec., Sat. 2:30-5pm | Wedgewood Park, 7201 W Wedgewood Dr, | Cookies, cocoa, and craft-making for the holidays. http://friendsofwedgewoodpark.org/event/holiday-celebration-tree-lighting/ | Free |

| DOG PHOTOS WITH SANTA (Wi 17) | | | |
|---|---|---|---|
| When? | Where? | Description and contact info | Admission |
| Early Dec., Sat., 9am-12pm | LaFollette Park, 9418 W Washington St, | Dog photo with Santa on CD with two photos. http://www.friendsoflafollettepark.com/events.html#photo_santa | $10 |

| CHRISTMAS TREE LIGHTING CEREMONY00CITY HALL (Wi 18) | | | |
|---|---|---|---|
| When? | Where? | Description and contact info | Admission |
| Mid Nov., Thu., 5pm | City Hall, 200 E. Wells | Tree lighting with Milwaukee mayor, and choir and theater performances. http://city.milwaukee.gov/home | Free |

| CANADIAN-PACIFIC HOLIDAY TRAIN STOP (Wi 19) | | | |
|---|---|---|---|
| **When?** | **Where?** | **Description and contact info** | **Admission** |
| Early Dec., see website for times | 433 W. St. Paul Ave., Depot | Festive train stop with live entertainment and food bank drive. https://www.facebook.com/HolidayTrain/ | Free, but donation of healthy food item appreciated |

| WINTER FEST AT JACKSON PARK (Wi 20) | | | |
|---|---|---|---|
| **When?** | **Where?** | **Description and contact info** | **Admission** |
| Mid Dec., Sat. 11am-3pm | Jackson Park, 3500 W. Forest Home Ave. | Face-painting, cocoa, crafts for kids, music, and more. http://county.milwaukee.gov/ParksCalendar | Free |

| HOLIDAY LIGHTS FESTIVAL (Wi 21) | | | |
|---|---|---|---|
| **When?** | **Where?** | **Description and contact info** | **Admission** |
| Late Nov. thru late Dec. | General downtown area | Hundreds of events, tours and lights celebrating winter holidays. http://www.milwaukeedowntown.com/about-us/special-events/milwaukee-holiday-lights-festival | Free |

| GINGERBREAD LAND—HOLIDAY SHOW (Wi 22) | | | |
|---|---|---|---|
| **When?** | **Where?** | **Description and contact info** | **Admission** |
| Early Jan. Sat., Sun. (see website for times) | Mitchell Park Domes, 524 S Layton Blvd. | Visit a gingerbread house covered in snowy frosting and candy canes and gum drops, among the poinsettias and decked holiday tree. http://county.milwaukee.gov/MitchellParkConserva10116.htm | $7 adults, $5 seniors, disabled, kids 6-17, free kids <6 |

- - - - - - - - - - - - - - - - - - - - - - - - - - - - - - - - - - - - - - - - -

| SANTA IN THE PARK--CUDAHY (Wi 23) | | | |
|---|---|---|---|
| **When?** | **Where?** | **Description and contact info** | **Admission** |
| Mid Dec., Sun. 12-3pm | Pulaski Park, 5400 S Swift Ave, Cudahy | Visits with Santa, treats, photos, and more. http://county.milwaukee.gov/ParksCalendar | Free |

| WAUWATOSA MERRY CHRISTMAS HOUSE--WAUWATOSA (Wi 24) | | | |
|---|---|---|---|
| **When?** | **Where?** | **Description and contact info** | **Admission** |
| Early Dec., Sat. & Sun. 1-4pm | Kneeland Walker House, 7406 Hillcrest Dr., Wauwatosa | A visit to the fabulous Kneeland Walker House all decked out in holiday mode, with warm cider and cookies. http://wauwatosahistoricalsociety.org/ | Free |

## CELTIC CHRISTMAS ARTS & CRAFTS SHOW--WAUWATOSA (Wi 25)

| When? | Where? | Description and contact info | Admission |
|---|---|---|---|
| Mid Nov., Sat. 9am-3:30 pm | Celtic Center, 1532 N. Wauwatosa Ave. | Show with large number of art/craft vendors for Irish gifts for holiday season. http://celticmke.com/CelticMKE-Events/Celtic-Boutique.htm | Free |

## CANADIAN-PACIFIC HOLIDAY TRAIN STOP--WAUWATOSA (Wi 26)

| When? | Where? | Description and contact info | Admission |
|---|---|---|---|
| Early Dec., see website for times | Harwood Ave. crossing | Festive train stop with live entertainment and food bank drive. https://www.facebook.com/HolidayTrain/ | Free, but donation of healthy food item appreciated |

## COMMUNITY-WIDE HANUKKAH CELEBRATION—WHITEFISH BAY (Wi 27)

| When? | Where? | Description and contact info | Admission |
|---|---|---|---|
| Early Dec., see website | Harry & Rose Samson Family Jewish Community Center, 6255 N. Santa Monica Blvd, Whitefish Bay | A great way to celebrate Hanukkah with lots of activities for children. www.jccmilwaukee.org | Free |

## BOERNER HOLIDAY GIFT FAIR WITH SANTA—HALES CORNERS (Wi 28)

| When? | Where? | Description and contact info | Admission |
|---|---|---|---|
| Early Dec., Sun. 10am-2pm | Boerner Botanical Gardens, 9400 Boerner Dr, Hales Corners | Visits with Santa and Mrs. Claus, musical entertainment, children's crafts and more. http://county.milwaukee.gov/ParksCalendar | Free |

## LITTLE WONDERS: WOODLAND HOLIDAYS--FRANKLIN (Wi 29)

| When? | Where? | Description and contact info | Admission |
|---|---|---|---|
| Early Dec., Mon. 9:30am-12pm | Wehr Nature Center, 9701 W College Ave, Franklin | Christmas-themed story and holiday treat. Get tickets at https://www.facebook.com/events/1726103904378623/ | $10 per child (with adult); $7 if Milw. Co. resident |

## CANADIAN-PACIFIC HOLIDAY TRAIN STOP--STURTEVANT (Wi 30)

| When? | Where? | Description and contact info | Admission |
|---|---|---|---|
| Early Dec., see website for times | 9900 E. Exploration Ct, Depot | Festive train stop with live entertainment and food bank drive. https://www.facebook.com/HolidayTrain/ | Free, but donation of healthy food item appreciated |

## EGYPTIAN COPTIC BAKE SALE—OAK CREEK (Wi 31)

| When? | Where? | Description and contact info | Admission |
|---|---|---|---|
| Mid Dec., Sat., Sun. 10am-6pm | St. Mary & St. Antonious Coptic Orthodox Church, 1521 W. Drexel Ave., Oak Creek | Christmas bake sale, ethnic food, church tour, Egyptian souvenirs. www.wiscopts.net | Families, couples, singles, seniors, free |

| CANADIAN-PACIFIC HOLIDAY TRAIN STOP--HARTLAND (Wi 32) | | | |
|---|---|---|---|
| **When?** | **Where?** | **Description and contact info** | **Admission** |
| Early Dec., see website for times | Parking lot adjacent to Cottonwood & Pawling | Festive train stop with live entertainment and food bank drive. https://www.facebook.com/HolidayTrain/ | Free, but donation of healthy food item appreciated |

| HANUKKAH STORYTIME WITH RABBI SHARI—BAYSHORE--GLENDALE (Wi 33) | | | |
|---|---|---|---|
| **When?** | **Where?** | **Description and contact info** | **Admission** |
| Late Dec., Wed. 1pm | Barnes & Noble Booksellers, Bayshore, 5755 N. Bayshore Dr., Glendale | Opportunity to join special guest Rabbi Shari and hear wonderful Hanukkah stories followed by a fun Hanukkah craft. http://milwaukee.eventful.com/events/hanukkah-storytime-rabbi-shari-/E0-001-096675227-1 | Free |

| ST. FRANCIS CHRISTMAS PARADE (Wi 34) | | | |
|---|---|---|---|
| **When?** | **Where?** | **Description and contact info** | **Admission** |
| Early Dec., Sun. 4:30pm | Starts at St. Francis Library, | Parade with drum line, poms, dancers, Santa and his helpers. https://www.facebook.com/CityofSaintFrancis/ | Free |

| WEST ALLIS CHRISTMAS PARADE (Wi 35) | | | |
|---|---|---|---|
| **When?** | **Where?** | **Description and contact info** | **Admission** |
| Early Dec., Sat., late afternoon | Greenfield Avenue, 81st to 65th, West Allis | Holiday floats, music, dancing. www.westalliswi.gov/calendar.aspx | Free |

# New Year's

| GLOW SKATE (Wi 36) | | | |
|---|---|---|---|
| **When?** | **Where?** | **Description and contact info** | **Admission** |
| Late Dec., Fri. 7:30-9pm | Wilson Park Arena, 4001 S 20th St, | Skating, glow-in-the-dark necklaces, holiday lights, music, prize drawings and a gourmet hot-chocolate bar (skate rentals available). http://county.milwaukee.gov/ParksCalendar | $5 |

# Valentine's Day

| VALENTINE'S DAY TOBOGGANING--WAUKESHA (Wi 37) | | | |
|---|---|---|---|
| **When?** | **Where?** | **Description and contact info** | **Admission** |
| Mid Feb., Sat., Sun. 1-4pm | Lowell Park, 2201 Michigan Ave., Waukesha | Bring own sled for a ride down the 350-ft. lighted chute, or rent one at the park (toboggan rentals are $10 an hour). Call (262) 522-9356 for up-to-date condition. | $9 daily pass if bring own toboggan |

# Dr. Martin Luther King Day

| MARTIN LUTHER KING CELEBRATION (Wi 38) | | | |
|---|---|---|---|
| **When?** | **Where?** | **Description and contact info** | **Admission** |
| Martin Luther King Day, 2:30 pm | Dr. Martin Luther King Jr. Community Center, 1531 W. Vliet St. | An afternoon in honor of Dr. King involving music, spoken work, and praise dance. http://county.milwaukee.gov/KingDayCelebration14707.htm | Free |

| DR. MARTIN LUTHER KING JR. CELEBRATION (Wi 39) | | | |
|---|---|---|---|
| **When?** | **Where?** | **Description and contact info** | **Admission** |
| Mid Jan., Sun. 1pm | Uihlein Hall 929 N. Water St. | Festivities and performances on the life and legacy of Dr. Martin Luther King. http://www.marcuscenter.org/ | Free |

# General

| FRENCH FILM FESTIVAL (Wi 40) | | | |
|---|---|---|---|
| **When?** | **Where?** | **Description and contact info** | **Admission** |
| Mid Feb., 10 days, see website | UW-Milwaukee Union Theatre 2200 East Kenwood Boulevard | (Subtitled) films in the French language—award winning, little known, classical, popular, and concessions available. http://uwm.edu/french-film-festival/ | Free |

| GALLERY NIGHT AND DAY (Wi 41) | | | |
|---|---|---|---|
| **When?** | **Where?** | **Description and contact info** | **Admission** |
| Late Jan., Fri. 5-9pm, Sat. 10am-4pm | Check web page. | Milwaukee's two-day premier art event for both the experienced art connoisseur and most beginning admirers that features 50 venues to explore throughout the downtown Milwaukee area four times a year. http://www.historicthirdward.org/events/gallerynight.php | Free |

| SLEDDING--PULASKI (Wi 42) | | | |
|---|---|---|---|
| **When?** | **Where?** | **Description and contact info** | **Admission** |
| Winter months, daytime, lighted evenings 4:30-8:30pm | Pulaski Park, 2701 S. 16th St. | Sledding day or night on lighted hill. http://county.milwaukee.gov/Sledding | Free |

| GUEST LECTURE SERIES ON THE ARTS (Wi 43) | | | |
|---|---|---|---|
| When? | Where? | Description and contact info | Admission |
| Winter, most Wed.'s 7:30-9pm | Art Center Lecture Hall, 2400 E. Kenwood Blvd. | Lectures on a variety of art-related topics including visual art, film, mythology, performance, story-telling, photography, and more. http://psoacal.uwm.edu/events/ | Free |

| MILWAUKEE COUNTY WINTER FARMERS MARKET (Wi 44) | | | |
|---|---|---|---|
| When? | Where? | Description and contact info | Admission |
| Dec. thru Feb. Sat. 9am-12:30pm | Mitchell Park Domes, 524 S. Layton Blvd. | Fresh produce, meat, eggs, dairy from Wisconsin small farms. http://www.mcwfm.org/ | Free |

| SLEDDING--WILSON (Wi 45) | | | |
|---|---|---|---|
| When? | Where? | Description and contact info | Admission |
| Winter, daytime | Wilson Recreation, 4001 S. 20th St. | Sledding hills for family and friends. http://county.milwaukee.gov/Sledding | Free |

| SLEDDING--MCGOVERN (Wi 46) | | | |
|---|---|---|---|
| When? | Where? | Description and contact info | Admission |
| Winter, daytime | McGovern Park, 5400 N. 51st St. | Sledding hills for family and friends. http://county.milwaukee.gov/Sledding | Free |

| SLEDDING--MCCARTY (Wi 47) | | | |
|---|---|---|---|
| When? | Where? | Description and contact info | Admission |
| Winter, daytime | McCarty Park, 8214 W. Cleveland Ave. | Sledding hills for family and friends. http://county.milwaukee.gov/Sledding | Free |

| ROLLER SKATING NIGHTS (Wi 48) | | | |
|---|---|---|---|
| When? | Where? | Description and contact info | Admission |
| Dec., every 3rd Fri. 6-8pm | Our Savior's Lutheran Church, 3022 W. Wisconsin Ave. | Roller skating and skate rentals. www.neighborhoodhousemke.org | Free with 2 non-perishable food items |

| OUTDOOR ICE SKATING—DOWNTOWN (Wi 49) | | | |
|---|---|---|---|
| When? | Where? | Description and contact info | Admission |
| Winter, only when ice is 6 inches thick | Red Arrow Park, 920 N Water St. | Ice skating for adults and children (heed "thin ice" signs). http://county.milwaukee.gov/OutdoorIceSkating11929.htm | Free |

| OUTDOOR ICE SKATING--RAINBOW (Wi 50) | | | |
|---|---|---|---|
| When? | Where? | Description and contact info | Admission |
| Winter, only when ice is 6 inches thick | Rainbow Land Rink 700 S. 119 St. | Ice skating for adults and children (heed "thin ice" signs. http://county.milwaukee.gov/OutdoorIceSkating11929.htm | Free |

## OUTDOOR ICE SKATING—BAY VIEW (Wi 51)

| When? | Where? | Description and contact info | Admission |
|---|---|---|---|
| Winter, only when ice is 6 inches thick | Humboldt Park, 3000 S Howell Ave. | Ice skating for adults and children (heed "thin ice" signs). http://county.milwaukee.gov/OutdoorIceSkating11929.htm | Free |

## OUTDOOR ICE SKATING—LAKE PARK (Wi 5)

| When? | Where? | Description and contact info | Admission |
|---|---|---|---|
| Winter, only when ice is 6 inches thick | Lake Park, 2975 N Lake Park Rd. | Ice skating for adults and children (heed "thin ice" signs). http://county.milwaukee.gov/OutdoorIceSkating11929.htm | Free |

## OUTDOOR ICE SKATING—LAFOLLETTE RINK (Wi 53)

| When? | Where? | Description and contact info | Admission |
|---|---|---|---|
| Winter, only when ice is 6 inches thick | LaFollette (land rink), 9418 W Washington St. | Ice skating for adults and children (heed "thin ice" signs. http://county.milwaukee.gov/OutdoorIceSkating11929.htm | Free |

## SATURDAY PRE-SCHOOL SERIES (Wi 54)

| When? | Where? | Description and contact info | Admission |
|---|---|---|---|
| Dec., select Sat.'s 10:30-11:30am | Riverside Park, 1500 E. Park Pl. | Chance for adults to bring children (ages 3-5) to enjoy nature with indoor or outdoor play. Requires registration. http://urbanecologycenter.org/programs-events-main.html | $7 adults, $5 kids |

## SLEDDING--LAFOLLETTE (Wi 55)

| When? | Where? | Description and contact info | Admission |
|---|---|---|---|
| Winter, daytime | LaFollette Park, 9418 W. Washington St. | Sledding hills for family and friends. http://county.milwaukee.gov/Sledding | Free |

## SLEDDING--GREEN (Wi 56)

| When? | Where? | Description and contact info | Admission |
|---|---|---|---|
| Winter, daytime | Green Park, 4235 S. Lipton Ave. | Sledding hills for family and friends. http://county.milwaukee.gov/Sledding | Free |

## SLEDDING--COLUMBUS (Wi 57)

| When? | Where? | Description and contact info | Admission |
|---|---|---|---|
| Winter, daytime | Columbus Park, 7301 W. Courtland Ave. | Sledding hills for family and friends. http://county.milwaukee.gov/Sledding | Free |

| SLEDDING--HUMBOLDT (Wi 58) | | | |
|---|---|---|---|
| When? | Where? | Description and contact info | Admission |
| Winter, daytime, evening | Humboldt Park, 3000 S. Howell Ave. | Sledding hills for family and friends, plus lighted sledding 4:30-8:30pm. http://county.milwaukee.gov/Sledding | Free |

| MARQUETTE GOLDEN EAGLES GAMES (Wi 59) | | | |
|---|---|---|---|
| When? | Where? | Description and contact info | Admission |
| Dec. thru late Feb. (regular season) | BMO Harris Bradley Center, 1001 N. 4th St. | Marquette University men's basketball games. http://www.gomarquette.com/tickets/m-baskbl-main.html | Some tickets at $5 and $10 |

| WOOLY BEAR FEST (Wi 60) | | | |
|---|---|---|---|
| When? | Where? | Description and contact info | Admission |
| Late Feb., Sat. 11am-3pm | River Revitalization Fdn., 2134 N. Riverboat Rd. | Chance to experience face painting, a log fire, light snacks, and friendly people, while demonstrating support for environmental restoration. It's free and family friendly. https://www.facebook.com/events/172891073072270/ | Free |

| MARQUETTE WOMEN'S BASKETBALL (Wi 61) | | | |
|---|---|---|---|
| When? | Where? | Description and contact info | Admission |
| Dec. thru late Feb. (regular season) | Al McGuire Center, 770 N. 12th St. | Marquette University women's basketball games. http://www.gomarquette.com/sports/w-baskbl/sched/marq-w-baskbl-sched.html | $5 and $10 |

| MILWAUKEE BUCKS GAMES (Wi 62) | | | |
|---|---|---|---|
|  | Where? | Description and contact info | Admission |
| Dec. thru Feb. (regular season) | BMO Harris Bradley Center, 1001 N. 4th St. | Games of Milwaukee Bucks of the National Basketball Association. http://www.nba.com/bucks/ | Some tickets at $9 and $10 |

| GLORIOUS GALAXIES (Wi 63) | | | |
|---|---|---|---|
| When? | Where? | Description and contact info | Admission |
| Mid Jan. thru late Feb., Fri.'s 7-7:55 pm | Manfred Olson Planetarium, UW-M Physics building, 1900 E. Kenwood Blvd. | Chance to explore other galaxies (over 170 million in existence). Explore shapes, collisions, and black holes. http://uwm.edu/planetarium/shows/special-events/ | $3 |

| CUPID'S CONSTELLATIONS (Wi 64) | | | |
|---|---|---|---|
| When? | Where? | Description and contact info | Admission |
| Mid Feb., Wed. 7-8pm | Manfred Olson Planetarium, UW-M Physics building, 1900 E. Kenwood Blvd. | One-night special showing of Cupid's Constellations, constellations in familiar patterns such as hearts, and tales of love including that of Princess Andromeda and Perseus. http://uwm.edu/planetarium/shows/special-events/ | $5 |

| WINTER SPORTS (Wi 65) | | | | |
|---|---|---|---|---|
| When? | Where? | Description and contact info | | Admission |
| Late Jan. one day (usually Sat.) 12-4pm | 1859 N. 40th St. | Family event sponsored by the Urban Ecology Center that includes a sled dog demonstration, ice skating, sledding, snowshoeing, cross-country skiing, arts and crafts and more. Register at http://urbanecologycenter.org/programs-events-main.html | | Free |

| ETHNIC FILMS (Wi 66/67) | | | |
|---|---|---|---|
| When? | Where? | Description and contact info | Admission |
| Select, Sundays, cold weather months, see website | Norway House,7507 W. Oklahoma Ave. | Czech and Slavic exceptional films with free ethnic treats. www.sokolmilwaukee.org | Free |

| ADULT OWL PROWL (Wi 68) | | | |
|---|---|---|---|
| When? | Where? | Description and contact info | Admission |
| Mid Jan. Fri., Sat. 7-9pm | Wehr Nature Center, 9701 W College Ave, Franklin, WI | An interactive program that highlights the habits and adaptations of our nocturnal neighbors. Register at http://www.friendsofwehr.org/winter-events/owl-prowl/ | $10 |

| WATERSTONE BANK ICE RINK (Wi 69) | | | |
|---|---|---|---|
| When? | Where? | Description and contact info | Admission |
| Opens mid Jan., sunrise-9pm | Center St. Park 6420 W. Clarke St. | Ice skating with warming house and free skate lending available at limited hours. See http://www.centerstreetpark.com/ice-rink | Free |

| PUBLIC ICE SKATING AT THE PETTIT (Wi 70) | | | |
|---|---|---|---|
| When? | Where? | Description and contact info | Admission |
| Winter, hours vary, see website | Pettit National Ice Center, 500 S. 84th St., | Indoor ice skating and skate rentals. http://thepettit.com/public-skate/ | $7.50, $6.50 kids 13-15, $5.50 kids 4-12 and seniors, free <4 |

| RUN/WALK TRACK AT THE PETTIT (Wi 71) | | | |
|---|---|---|---|
| When? | Where? | Description and contact info | Admission |
| Winter, hours vary, see website | Pettit National Ice Center, 500 S. 84th St. | Walk or run on 430 meter track with lockers and showers for $1 extra at limited times. http://thepettit.com/sports/run-walk-track/ | $4 day pass |

## MUSIC UNDER GLASS (Wi 72)

| When? | Where? | Description and contact info | Admission |
|---|---|---|---|
| Mid Jan.- mid Mar. Thu.'s 6:30-9pm | Mitchell Park Domes, 524 S Layton Blvd. | Live music and legendary stars. http://county.milwaukee.gov/FloralShowampEventSc 10360/MusicUnderGlass.htm | $5 adults, free kids <12 |

## FAMILY FREE DAY AT THE ZOO (Wi 73)

| When? | Where? | Description and contact info | Admission |
|---|---|---|---|
| Early Dec., Jan., Feb., select Sat.'s 9:30am-4:30pm | Milwaukee County Zoo, 10001 W. Bluemound Rd. | If you want to stay warm, we have many indoor animal exhibits for your enjoyment. If you're more of the outdoorsy type, you'll also find many outdoor animal exhibits. http://www.milwaukeezoo.org/events/ | Free |

## WINTERFEST FOR AFTERNOON NAPPERS (Wi 74)

| When? | Where? | Description and contact info | Admission |
|---|---|---|---|
| Late Jan. 10:30am-12pm, see website for dates | Washington Park 1859 N. 40th St. | Opportunity for children ages 5 and under accompanied of adult to enjoy a morning of fun including a craft, hike and puppet show and still get home in time for afternoon nap. Register at http://urbanecologycenter.org/programs-events-main.html | $7, $5 kids (with adult) |

## SLEDDING THE SLOPES OF MENOMONEE VALLEY (Wi 75)

| When? | Where? | Description and contact info | Admission |
|---|---|---|---|
| Late Jan. Tue. 4-6pm | Menomonee Valley 3700 W. Pierce | An evening of snow and sledding in Three Bridges Park with hot chocolate (if there is no snow, will hike Three Bridges Park). Register at http://urbanecologycenter.org/programs-events-main.html | Free |

## OWL PROWL FOR FAMILIES (Wi 76)

| When? | Where? | Description and contact info | Admission |
|---|---|---|---|
| Late Jan. Tue. 6-7:30pm | Riverside Park 1500 E. Park Pl. | Educational hike through Riverside Park to listen for nocturnal creatures (includes hot chocolate). Register at http://urbanecologycenter.org/programs-events-main.html | $9 adults, kids $6 |

## CROSS COUNTRY SKIING FOR KIDS (Wi 77)

| When? | Where? | Description and contact info | Admission |
|---|---|---|---|
| Late Jan. Thu. 4-6pm | Menomonee Valley 3700 W. Pierce | Bring children to workshop designed just for kids to learn all they need to know before hitting the slopes, with gear provided. Register at http://urbanecologycenter.org/programs-events-main.html | $5 kids 7-12 |

## SKYWAUKEE WALKING TOUR (Wi 78)

| When? | Where? | Description and contact info | Admission |
|---|---|---|---|
| Jan. 9-end of winter, Sat. 1pm | Meets in the street level lobby of the Plankinton Building, 161 W. Wisconsin Ave. | Historic Milwaukee Inc. tour that explores the architectural and cultural history of Milwaukee's landmarks while staying indoors;. http://historicmilwaukee.org/walking-tours/ | $10 adults; $2 kids 7-17, free kids under 7 |

| GINGERBREAD LAND—HOLIDAY SHOW (Wi 79) | | | |
|---|---|---|---|
| When? | Where? | Description and contact info | Admission |
| Early Jan. Sat., Sun. (see website for times) | Mitchell Park Domes, 524 S Layton Blvd. | Visit a gingerbread house covered in snowy frosting and candy canes and gum drops, among the poinsettias and decked holiday tree. http://county.milwaukee.gov/MitchellParkConserva10116.htm | $7 adults, $5 seniors, disabled, kids 6-17, free kids <6 |

■■■■■■■■■■■■■■■■■■■■■■■■■■■■■■■■■■■■■■■■■■■■■■■■■■■■■■■

| WAUKESHA JAMBOREE (Wi 80) | | | |
|---|---|---|---|
| When? | Where? | Description and contact info | Admission |
| Mid Jan., Fri. thru Sun. | Opening ceremonies at Lowell Park, 2201 Michigan Ave, Waukesha | Event features over 35 winter events ranging from ice sculpting contests to ice bocce ball to ice skating to ice hockey expo to giant slide. http://www.janboree.org/ | Free |

| SLEDDING—BROWN DEER (Wi 81) | | | |
|---|---|---|---|
| When? | Where? | Description and contact info | Admission |
| Winter, daytime | Brown Deer Park, 7835 N. Green Bay Rd. | Sledding hills for family and friends. http://county.milwaukee.gov/Sledding | Free |

| OUTDOOR ICE SKATING--CUDAHY (Wi 82/83) | | | |
|---|---|---|---|
| When? | Where? | Description and contact info | Admission |
| Winter, only when ice is 6 inches thick | Sheridan Park, 4800 S. Lake Dr., Cudahy | Ice skating for adults and children (heed "thin ice" signs). http://county.milwaukee.gov/OutdoorIceSkating11929.htm | Free |

| ICE FISHING & WINTER SPORTS SHOW—WEST ALLIS (Wi 84) | | | |
|---|---|---|---|
| When? | Where? | Description and contact info | Admission |
| Early Dec., Fri. 12-7pm; Sat. 10am-7pm, Sun. 9am-2pm | Wisconsin State Fair Park, 640 S. 84th, West Allis | Rows of exhibits with products and services dedicated to the ice fishing and winter sports enthusiast. http://wistatefair.com/wsfp/events/ | Free |

| SLEDDING--FRANKLIN (Wi 85) | | | |
|---|---|---|---|
| When? | Where? | Description and contact info | Admission |
| Winter, daytime, evening | Whitnall Park, 5879 S. 92nd St., Franklin | Sledding hills for family and friends, concessions, plus lighted sledding 4:30-8:30pm. http://county.milwaukee.gov/Sledding | Free |

## HMONG NEW YEAR—WEST ALLIS (Wi 86)

| When? | Where? | Description and contact info | Admission |
|---|---|---|---|
| Early Dec., Sat., Sun. 8am-5pm | State Fair Park Expo Center; 8200 W. Greenfield Ave., West Allis | Celebration marks the end of the Hmong harvest season, which ends on November 31, and a time of several days of music, singing, dancing, games, and food. http://wistatefair.com/wsfp/events/ | Adults $3; free seniors, kids <12 fr |

## WONDERFUL WORLD OF WEDDINGS—WEST ALLIS (Wi 87)

| When? | Where? | Description and contact info | Admission |
|---|---|---|---|
| Early Jan., Sat., Sun. 10am-4:30pm | State Fair Park Expo Center; 8200 W. Greenfield Ave., West Allis | The latest trends in wedding gowns, tuxedos, photographers, florists, music, sample wedding cakes and food tastings, over 100 exhibitors. www.WisconsinWeddingShow.com | $10, $8.50 seniors, $8 military, free kids <13 |

## MILWAUKEE BOAT SHOW—WEST ALLIS (Wi 88)

| When? | Where? | Description and contact info | Admission |
|---|---|---|---|
| Mid Jan., one week, two weekends (except Mon & Tue) | State Fair Park Expo Center; 8200 W. Greenfield Ave., West Allis | Wisconsin's largest boat show with over 400 boats from over 80 manufacturers, yachts, aluminum fishing boats, ski boats, pontoons, runabouts & jet skis, plus dock systems & marine accessories. www.milwaukeeboatshow.com | $10, free kids <13 with adult |

## GREAT LAKES PET EXPO—WEST ALLIS (Wi 89)

| When? | Where? | Description and contact info | Admission |
|---|---|---|---|
| Late Jan. 1-5pm | State Fair Park Expo Center; 8200 W. Greenfield Ave., West Allis | Wisconsin's largest charitable event that raises money for companion animals in Wisconsin. Featuring exhibitors including local Wisconsin rescues, pet products and services, great entertainment, and the best shopping for pet lovers. www.petexpomilwaukee.com/ | $6. Free kids <13 & military w/ID |

## OUTDOOR ICE SKATING— HALES CORNERS (Wi 90)

| When? | Where? | Description and contact info | Admission |
|---|---|---|---|
| Winter, only when ice is 6 inches thick | Alyson Dudek International Ice Center, 5765 S New Berlin Rd. Hales Corners | Ice skating for adults and children (heed "thin ice" signs). http://county.milwaukee.gov/OutdoorIceSkating11929.htm | Free |

## OUTDOOR ICE SKATING—WEST ALLIS (Wi 91)

| When? | Where? | Description and contact info | Admission |
|---|---|---|---|
| Winter, only when ice is 6 inches thick | McCarty Park, 8214 W. Cleveland Ave. | Ice skating for adults and children (heed "thin ice" signs). http://county.milwaukee.gov/OutdoorIceSkating11929.htm | Free |

| OUTDOOR ICE SKATING-GREENDALE (Wi 92) | | | |
|---|---|---|---|
| When? | Where? | Description and contact info | Admission |
| Winter, only when ice is 6 inches thick | Scout Lake , 5902 W Loomis Rd., Greendale | Ice skating for adults and children (heed "thin ice" signs). http://county.milwaukee.gov/OutdoorIceSkating11929.htm | Free |

| OUTDOOR ICE SKATING--WAUWATOSA (Wi 93) | | | |
|---|---|---|---|
| When? | Where? | Description and contact info | Admission |
| Winter, only when ice is 6 inches thick | Waterstone Bank Rink, 6420 W Clarke St., Wauwatosa | Ice skating for adults and children (heed "thin ice" signs). http://county.milwaukee.gov/OutdoorIceSkating11929.htm | Free |

| WOMAN UP!—WEST ALLIS (Wi 94) | | | |
|---|---|---|---|
| When? | Where? | Description and contact info | Admission |
| Early Feb. Sat. 10am-4pm | State Fair Park Expo Center; 8200 W. Greenfield Ave., West Allis | A day to celebrate all walks of a woman's life with 250+ vendors and experts in health care, fitness, finance, beauty, education and food as you shop, sample, and listen to presentations. www.shepherdexpress.com/womanup | $7 |

| SLEDDING—HALES CORNERS (Wi 95) | | | |
|---|---|---|---|
| When? | Where? | Description and contact info | Admission |
| Winter, daytime | Hales Corners Park, 5765 S. New Berlin Rd. | Sledding hills for family and friends. http://county.milwaukee.gov/Sledding | Free |

| MILWAUKEE/NARI SPRING IMPROVEMENT SHOW—WEST ALLIS (Wi 96) | | | |
|---|---|---|---|
| When? | Where? | Description and contact info | Admission |
| Mid Feb. Thu-Sun., 12-8pm | State Fair Park Expo Center; 8200 W. Greenfield Ave., West Allis | Home improvement trade show with special attractions and interactive entertainment. www.milwaukeenari.org | $10. $8 seniors, free kids <16 & military w/ID |

| MILWAUKEE RV SHOW—WEST ALLIS (Wi 97) | | | |
|---|---|---|---|
| When? | Where? | Description and contact info | Admission |
| Late Feb. Thu. thru Sun., see hours on website | State Fair Park Expo Center; 8200 W. Greenfield Ave., West Allis | Displays and sales of a wide range of recreational vehicles including pop-up campers, travel trailers, 5th wheels and motorhomes. www.milwaukeervshow.com | $8, $7 seniors, free kids <13 |

| SLEDDING--WAUWATOSA (Wi 98) | | | |
|---|---|---|---|
| When? | Where? | Description and contact info | Admission |
| Winter, daytime, evening | Currie Park, 3535 N. Mayfair Rd. | Sledding hills for family and friends, plus lighted sledding 4:30-8:30pm. http://county.milwaukee.gov/Sledding | Free |

# Spring: March, April, May (not in chronological order)

> Listings do NOT include classes, workouts, or clubs
>
> LISTINGS ONLY INCLUDE RECURRING EVENTS UNDER $10 PER ADULT ADMISSION. THE ADMISSION PRICE ONLY COVERS THE ENTRANCE FEES AND DOES NOT INCLUDE THE PRICE OF FOOD, RIDES, GOODS, RAFFLE TICKETS, OR OTHER ITEMS THAT MAY BE PART OF THE EVENT.
>
> PLEASE ALWAYS CHECK THE CONTACT INFO FOR ANY RECENT CHANGES IN THESE EVENTS.

## National Holiday-Specific

## St. Patrick's Day

| ST. PATRICK'S DAY PARADE (Sp 1) | | | |
|---|---|---|---|
| When? | Where? | Description and contact info | Admission |
| Mid Mar., Sat. begins at noon | Begins in front of Grand Ave. Mall, west on Kilbourn to Old World Third | Parade of marching bands, Irish dancers, floats, Irish dignitaries. http://www.shamrockclubwis.com/page9.html | Free |

| POST ST. PATRICK'S DAY PARADE PARTY (Sp 2) | | | |
|---|---|---|---|
| When? | Where? | Description and contact info | Admission |
| Mid Mar., Sat. 1:30-5pm | Irish Cultural Heritage Center, 2133 W. Wisconsin Ave. | Live entertainment, children's activities, leprechaun stories, and more http://www.shamrockclubwis.com/page9.html | Free |

| IRISHMAN'S WALK--PLYMOUTH (Sp 3) | | | |
|---|---|---|---|
| When? | Where? | Description and contact info | Admission |
| March 17 (see website for hours) | Eastern Avenue, Plymouth | Walk for Irish and non-Irish on Eastern Avenue ending at 52 Stafford in downtown Plymouth, where the festivities continue with Irish food, live music and beverages. http://plymouthwisconsin.com/family.html | Free |

## Easter

| WASHINGTON HEIGHTS EASTER EGG HUNT (Sp 4) | | | |
|---|---|---|---|
| When? | Where? | Description and contact info | Admission |
| Mid Mar., Sat. 11:45am-1pm | Washington Park, W. Vliet St. & N. 40th St. | Fun event for children and adults with Easter egg hunt. http://whna.net/event/easter-egg-hunt-2016-03-28/ | Free |

| EASTER BUNNY AT NORTHPOINT LIGHTHOUSE (Sp 5) | | | |
|---|---|---|---|
| **When?** | **Where?** | **Description and contact info** | **Admission** |
| Mid Mar., Sat. 1-4pm | Northpoint Lighthouse, 2650 N. Wahl Ave. | Easter bunny appearance at museum with historic and maritime significance. http://northpointlighthouse.org/events/month/ | $8, $5 seniors & kids 5-11, free kids<4 |

| LAFOLLETTE PARK PANCAKE BREAKFAST AND EGG HUNT (Sp 6) | | | |
|---|---|---|---|
| **When?** | **Where?** | **Description and contact info** | **Admission** |
| Late Mar., Sat. 8am-12pm | LaFollette Park, 9418 West Washington St. | Breakfast at 8-10:30 am; egg hunt at 11am. http://friendsoflafollettepark.com/events.html | Free |

- - - - - - - - - - - - - - - - - - - - - - - - - - - - - - - - - - - - - - - - -

| EASTER BUNNY AT PULASKI--CUDAHY (Sp 7) | | | |
|---|---|---|---|
| **When?** | **Where?** | **Description and contact info** | **Admission** |
| Late Mar., 12-3pm | Pulaski Park, 5400 S Swift Ave, Cudahy | Bunny sitting for photos, bake sale, and family-priced hot dog lunch. https://www.facebook.com/groups/851254978225815/ | Free |

| EASTER DAY EVENT—HALES CORNERS (Sp 8) | | | |
|---|---|---|---|
| **When?** | **Where?** | **Description and contact info** | **Admission** |
| Easter, 10am-2pm | Boerner Botanical Gardens, 9400 Boerner Dr, Hales Corners | A visit with the Easter Bunny, balloon animal from Sparkle the Clown, and craft activities for kids all morning & afternoon. http://www.opentable.com/boerner-botanical-gardens | Free |

| BUDDY SQUIRREL ANNUAL EASTER OPEN HOUSE—ST. FRANCIS (Sp 9) | | | |
|---|---|---|---|
| **When?** | **Where?** | **Description and contact info** | **Admission** |
| Mid Mar., Sun. 9am-3pm | 1801 E. Bolivar Ave., St. Francis, | Opportunity to see how Milwaukee's "Original Whipped Crème Eggs" are made, meet Mr. & Mrs. Easter Bunny and "Buddy Squirrel." https://www.facebook.com/BuddySquirrel/ | Free |

# Memorial Day

| MEMORIAL DAY PARADE (Sp 10) | | | |
|---|---|---|---|
| **When?** | **Where?** | **Description and contact info** | **Admission** |
| Memorial Day, Mon., 2-4pm | Starting at 4th St. and Wisconsin Ave., | Parade honoring US veterans, starting at 4th and Wisconsin Avenue and ending at War Memorial Center. http://www.war-veterans.org/Parade.htm | Free |

| THE MAGGIANO'S LITTLE ITALY FAMILY KITE FESTIVAL (Sp 11) | | | |
|---|---|---|---|
| **When?** | **Where?** | **Description and contact info** | **Admission** |
| Late May, Sat. 10am-6pm, Sun. 10am-5pm | Veterans Park, 1010 N Lincoln Memorial Dr. | A Memorial Day weekend festival of major kite performers, food, and Kids Mad Dash. http://www.giftofwings.com/events/familykitefest/ | Free |

| WORKERS' MEMORIAL DAY (Sp 12) | | | |
|---|---|---|---|
| **When?** | **Where?** | **Description and contact info** | **Admission** |
| Late Apr., Thu. 4:30-7:30pm | Zeidler Union Square, 633 W Wisconsin Ave #409 | An event of the Milwaukee Area Labor Council. http://www.milwaukeelabor.org/event_caledar/ | Free |

■■■■■■■■■■■■■■■■■■■■■■■■■■■■■■■■■■■■■■■■■■■■■■■■■■■■

| CORN & BRAT ROAST—EAST TROY (Sp 13) | | | |
|---|---|---|---|
| **When?** | **Where?** | **Description and contact info** | **Admission** |
| Late May, Fri. 4-8pm, Sat. 11am-6pm, Sun. 11am-6pm, Mon. 11am-5pm | East Troy Village Square, East Troy | Memorial Day long weekend of food including community-wide rummage sale, live entertainment, and more. https://easttroy.org/news/2016/ | Free |

| CHOCOLATE FEST--BURLINGTON (Sp 14) | | | |
|---|---|---|---|
| **When?** | **Where?** | **Description and contact info** | **Admission** |
| Late May, Thu.5—10pm, Fri.4pm-12am, Sat.10-12am, Sun. 10-12am, Mon. 11am-7pm | Burlington Festival Park, Burlington | Long Memorial Day weekend of games, rides, music, fireworks, cooking demonstrations, and of course, chocolate. http://www.chocolatefest.com/ | $8, $3 kids 5-12, free kids <5 |

# General

| BAVARIAN MAIFEST (Sp 15) | | | |
|---|---|---|---|
| **When?** | **Where?** | **Description and contact info** | **Admission** |
| Early May, Thu. thru Sun | Estabrook Park, 4600 N. Estabrook Dr. | Bavarian celebration for arrival of spring; dancing, music, food, playground, contests. Info@estabrookbeergarden.com | Free |

| WEST SIDE ART WALK (Sp 16) | | | |
|---|---|---|---|
| **When?** | **Where?** | **Description and contact info** | **Admission** |
| Late Apr., Fri., Sat., 10am-4pm | W. Vliet St. between 54th & 60th Sts. | Locally-owned galleries and shops that feature an array of Milwaukee-made artwork, plus other shopping options. http://www.westvlietstreet.org/ | Free |

| MILWAUKEE COUNTY WINTER FARMERS MARKET (Sp 17) | | | |
|---|---|---|---|
| **When?** | **Where?** | **Description and contact info** | **Admission** |
| Mar.-early Apr., Sat. 9am-12:30pm | Mitchell Park Domes, 524 S. Layton Blvd. | Fresh produce, meat, eggs, dairy from Wisconsin small farms. http://www.mcwfm.org/ | Free |

| GARDEN IMPRESSIONS SPRING FLORAL SHOW AT THE DOMES (Sp 18) | | | |
|---|---|---|---|
| When? | Where? | Description and contact info | Admission |
| May, 9am-5pm, see website | Mitchell Park Horticultural Conservatory, 524 S Layton Blvd. | The experience of a spring garden as an outdoor art gallery in the Show Domes amongst the brilliant tulips, Easter lilies, hydrangeas and marigolds, including easels displaying paintings of the domes done in the styles of Monet, Cezanne, and Van Gogh. http://county.milwaukee.gov/MitchellParkConserva10116.htm | Free at 9am-12pm Mon.'s |

| GALLERY NIGHT AND DAY (Sp 19) | | | |
|---|---|---|---|
| When? | Where? | Description and contact info | Admission |
| Late Apr. Fri. 5-9pm, Sat. 10am-4pm | Check web page. | Milwaukee's two-day premier art event for both the experienced art connoisseur and most beginning admirers that features 50 venues to explore throughout the downtown Milwaukee area four times a year. http://www.historicthirdward.org/events/gallerynight.php | Free |

| GARDEN DISTRICT CRAFT FAIR (Sp 20) | | | |
|---|---|---|---|
| When? | Where? | Description and contact info | Admission |
| Late Apr., Sat. 9am-3pm | 3333 S. Howell Ave. | Fair of over 25 vendors, concessions, prizes, bake sale, and more. http://www.milwaukeegdna.com/ | $1 |

| SATURDAY PRE-SCHOOL SERIES (Sp 21) | | | |
|---|---|---|---|
| When? | Where? | Description and contact info | Admission |
| May, select Sat.'s 10:30-11:30am | Riverside Park, 1500 E. Park Pl. | Chance for adults to bring children (ages 3-5) to enjoy nature with indoor or outdoor play. Requires registration. http://urbanecologycenter.org/programs-events-main.html | $7 adults, $5 kids |

| OPEN ROCK CLIMBING (Sp 22) | | | |
|---|---|---|---|
| When? | Where? | Description and contact info | Admission |
| May, 1st Sun. of month 2-4pm | Riverside Park 1500 E. Park Pl. | One free climbing session with the possibility for additional climbs if time allows. http://urbanecologycenter.org/programs-events-main.html | Free, donations welcome |

| RENT A BIKE AT VETERANS PARK (Sp 23) | | | |
|---|---|---|---|
| When? | Where? | Description and contact info | Admission |
| Mid Apr. thru May, Sat.'s, Sun.'s, late am to sunset | Veterans Park, 1400 N. Lincoln Memorial Dr. | Bicycle riding along Milwaukee's lakefront. http://www.wheelfunrentals.com/Locations/Milwaukee-2 | $10 adults bikes (cruiser or mountain); $5 kids' bikes |

| OPEN HOUSE—ST. FRANCIS DE SALES SEMINARY (Sp 24) | | | |
|---|---|---|---|
| When? | Where? | Description and contact info | Admission |
| Late Apr., Sun. 11am (mass), 12-2pm (tour) | 3257 S. Lake Dr. | Opportunity to experience a Milwaukee landmark through mass and tour of seminary. https://www.sfs.edu/OpenHouse | Free |

## MILWAUKEE UNDERGROUND FILM FEST (Sp 25)

| When? | Where? | Description and contact info | Admission |
|---|---|---|---|
| Early May, Thu.-Sun., see website for schedule | Helene Zelazo Center for the Performing Arts, 2419 E. Kenwood Blvd. | A student-run, international film festival dedicated to showcasing contemporary works of film and video that innovate in form, technique, and content. http://film-milwaukee.org/ | Free |

## STUDENT FILM AND VIDEO FESTIVAL (Sp 26)

| When? | Where? | Description and contact info | Admission |
|---|---|---|---|
| Mid May, Fri. 7-10pm | UWM Union Cinema, 2400 E. Kenwood Blvd. | A juried showcase of the best short films and videos from the pioneering UWM Department of Film, Video, Animation, and New Genres. http://uwm.edu/studentinvolvement/tag/student-film-and-video-festival/ | Free |

## FAMILY HIKE (Sp 27)

| When? | Where? | Description and contact info | Admission |
|---|---|---|---|
| Mar. & Apr, Tue.'s 4-6pm | Menomonee Valley, 3700 W. Pierce St. | Guided hike to see changes in seasons through Three Bridges Park. http://urbanecologycenter.org/programs-events-main.html | Free, but might need to register |

## UWM'S LATIN AMERICAN FILM SERIES (Sp 28)

| When? | Where? | Description and contact info | Admission |
|---|---|---|---|
| Early Apr., one week, see website for times | Union Theatre, 2200 E. Kenwood Blvd. | Films including international award winners from countries throughout Latin America, in Spanish, Portuguese, English, and Kaqchikel Maya, with subtitles where needed. http://www4.uwm.edu/clacs/filmseries/filmseries38.cfm | Free |

## FONDY FARMERS MARKET (Sp 29)

| When? | Where? | Description and contact info | Admission |
|---|---|---|---|
| May, Sat. 9am-12pm | 2200 W. Fond du Lac Ave. | Fresh produce from Wisconsin farmers, baked goods, arts, crafts, activities. http://fondymarket.org/ | Free |

## MAPLE SUGARING AT RIVERSIDE (Sp 30)

| When? | Where? | Description and contact info | Admission |
|---|---|---|---|
| Late Apr., Sat. 10am-2pm | Riverside Park, 1449 E. Park Pl. | An in-depth look at maple sugar sap harvesting, presented by Urban Ecology Center. Register at http://urbanecologycenter.org/programs-events-main.html | Free |

## CZECH/SLOVAK GYMNASTICS EXHIBITION (Sp 31)

| When? | Where? | Description and contact info | Admission |
|---|---|---|---|
| Spring, see website | Norway House, 7507 W. Oklahoma Ave. | Chance to see youth gymnasts sponsored by Milwaukee Sokol demonstrate their physical fitness skills and compete for metals. www.sokolmilwaukee.org. | Free |

| MILWAUKEE BUCKS GAMES (Sp 32) | | | |
|---|---|---|---|
| | Where? | Description and contact info | Admission |
| Mar-mid Apr. (regular season) | BMO Harris Bradley Center, 1001 N. 4th St. | Games of Milwaukee Bucks of the National Basketball Association. http://www.nba.com/bucks/ | Some tickets at $9 and $10 |

| HAPPY BIRTHDAY DR. SEUSS (Sp 33) | | | |
|---|---|---|---|
| When? | Where? | Description and contact info | Admission |
| Early Mar., Sat., 10am-1pm | MPL Central Library, 814 W. Wisconsin Ave. | Opportunity to celebrate all things Seuss with games, stories, a fish pond, cookie decorating, live entertainment, crafts, and live animals. http://www.mpl.org/services/events/ | Free |

| CANTOS DE LAS AMERICAS (Sp 34) | | | |
|---|---|---|---|
| When? | Where? | Description and contact info | Admission |
| Late Apr., Fri., 6:30pm | Marcus Center for the Arts, Uihlein Hall, 929 N Water St. | Concert by MPS students performing songs and dances from the Caribbean, Africa, indigenous America, Latin America and Europe (in addition to the Hmong, Laotian cultures). http://www.marcuscenter.org/calendar/month/ | Free |

| FAMILY FREE DAY AT THE ZOO (Sp 35) | | | |
|---|---|---|---|
| When? | Where? | Description and contact info | Admission |
| Early Mar., select Sat. 9:30am-4:30pm | Milwaukee County Zoo, 10001 W. Bluemound Rd. | If you want to stay warm, we have many indoor animal exhibits for your enjoyment. If you're more of the outdoorsy type, you'll also find many outdoor animal exhibits. http://www.milwaukeezoo.org/events/ | Free |

| WARBLER WALKS IN LAKE PARK (Sp 36) | | | |
|---|---|---|---|
| When? | Where? | Description and contact info | Admission |
| Late May, Sat.'s, 8am-10am | 2975 N Lake Park Rd. (meet at the Warming House) | Informal walks that are open to the general public of all ages, led by recreational birders familiar with Lake Park. http://lakeparkfriends.org/event/warbler-walks/?instance_id=177 | Free |

| FAMILY KITE FESTIVAL (Sp 37) | | | |
|---|---|---|---|
| When? | Where? | Description and contact info | Admission |
| Late May, Sat., 9am-6pm | Veterans Park, 1010 N Lincoln Memorial Dr. | Festival featuring the Fast Track Oil Centers Grand Launch of 500 kites, the Kids Mad Dash, and entertainment. http://county.milwaukee.gov/ParksCalendar | Free |

| ESCUELA VERDE'S COMMUNITY NIGHT (Sp 38) | | | |
|---|---|---|---|
| When? | Where? | Description and contact info | Admission |
| Mid Mar., Tue. 5-7pm | Escuela Verde School, 3828 W. Pierce St. | An evening of music, food, karaoke, bake sale. http://www.escuelaverde.org/ | Free |

| MILWAUKEE MUSLIM FILM FESTIVAL (Sp 39) | | | |
|---|---|---|---|
| When? | Where? | Description and contact info | Admission |
| Early Mar. thru late Apr. | Milwaukee Art Museum, 700 N. Art Museum Drive; Oriental Theater, 2230 N. Farwell Ave.; Student Union (2nd Fl.), 2200 E. Kenwood Blvd. | Films that explore topics that are timely, relevant, and generate meaningful discussion about Muslims and the Muslim world. http://mmfilmfest.com/ | $8, student discounts where applicable |

| ROOT RIVER HIKE & BIKE (Sp 40) | | | |
|---|---|---|---|
| When? | Where? | Description and contact info | Admission |
| Late Apr., Sat. 7am-4pm | Greenfield Park, 2028 S. 124th St. | A scenic and healthy program with plenty of outdoor exercise. http://badgertrails.org/upcoming-events/root-river-hike/ | Free |

| NATURE NAUTS: CRAZY OVER CRANES--FRANKLIN (Sp 41) | | | |
|---|---|---|---|
| When? | Where? | Description and contact info | Admission |
| Early Apr., Sun. 1-2 pm | Wehr Nature Center, 9701 W College Ave, Franklin | Program for kids 4-6 to discover how they compare to Wisconsin's tallest bird, learn to talk like a crane, do the crane dance, and find out what it takes to raise a baby crane. http://www.friendsofwehr.org/childrens-programs/early-childhood/ | $10 child; $7 Milw. County residents |

| BROOKFIELD FARMERS MARKET (Sp 42) | | | |
|---|---|---|---|
| When? | Where? | Description and contact info | Admission |
| May., Sat. 7:30am-12pm | 2000 N. Calhoun Rd. | Fresh produce from Wisconsin farmers; arts/crafts fair every third Sun. of month. http://www.brookfieldfarmersmarket.com/ | Free |

| FAMILY EVENT: MAKE YOUR OWN FAIRY OR GNOME GARDEN—HALES CORNERS (Sp 43) | | | |
|---|---|---|---|
| When? | Where? | Description and contact info | Admission |
| Mid Mar., Sat. 10am-12pm | Boerner Botanical Gardens, 9400 Boerner Dr, Hales Corners | Chance to create a fairy or gnome garden for the home using miniature plants and other tiny elements (materials provided). ttp://boernerbotanicalgardens.org/events/ | Free |

| PEWAUKEE LAKE WATER SKI CLUB SHOW--PEWAUKEE (Sp 44) | | | |
|---|---|---|---|
| When? | Where? | Description and contact info | Admission |
| Late May, Thu.'s 6:45pm; some Sat.'s & Mon.'s 5:30pm | Lakefront Park, Pewaukee | Show of skilled water skiing on beautiful lake. http://plwsc.org/ | Free |

| MENOMONEE FALLS FARMERS MARKET (Sp 45) | | | |
|---|---|---|---|
| When? | Where? | Description and contact info | Admission |
| May, Wed. 8am-3pm | North Junior HS parking lot, Main St. (one block west of Appleton Ave.) | Fresh produce from Wisconsin farmers, baked goods, arts, crafts. http://menomoneefallsdowntown.com/ | Free |


| COMMUNITY STREET FESTIVAL—PORT WASHINGTON (Sp 46) | | | |
|---|---|---|---|
| When? | Where? | Description and contact info | Admission |
| Late May, Sun. 12-5pm | Grand Ave. and Franklin St., Port Washington | Festival of live music, children's activities, food, and over 80 vendors. https://www.facebook.com/Port-Washington-Main-Street-148006119068/ | Free |


| WEST ALLIS FARMERS MARKET (Sp 47) | | | |
|---|---|---|---|
| When? | Where? | Description and contact info | Admission |
| May, Tue. 12-6pm, Sat. 1-6pm | 6501 W. National Ave. | Fresh produce from Wisconsin farmers; baked goods, arts, crafts. https://www.facebook.com/westallisfarmersmarket/ | Free |


| IMMACULATE HEART OF MARY FESTIVAL—WEST ALLIS (Sp 48) | | | |
|---|---|---|---|
| When? | Where? | Description and contact info | Admission |
| Late May, Fri. opens 4:30pm, Sat. opens 4:30pm, Sun. opens 11:30am | 1121 S. 116th St., West Allis | Festival including bands, food, tents, rides, games, raffle, and more. https://www.facebook.com/ihmwestallis | Free |


| FAMILY FROG FROLIC—FRANKLIN (Sp 49) | | | |
|---|---|---|---|
| When? | Where? | Description and contact info | Admission |
| Late Apr., Fri. 7-9pm | Wehr Nature Center, 9701 W College Ave, Franklin | Program for kids 5 and older to meet Wisconsin amphibians up close and then stroll out to the ponds of Wehr to listen for the spring sounds. of frogs chorusing. http://www.friendsofwehr.org/spring-events/family-frog-frolics/ | Free |


| DAN JANSEN FAMILY FEST--GREENFIELD (Sp 50) | | | |
|---|---|---|---|
| When? | Where? | Description and contact info | Admission |
| Late May, Fri. 5-11pm, Sat. 12-11pm, Sun. 12-4pm | Konkel Park, 5151 W. Layton Ave., Greenfield | Festival of rides, car show, live entertainment, and more. http://jansenfest.org/ | Free |


| MAPLE SUGAR DAYS--FRANKLIN (Sp 51) | | | |
|---|---|---|---|
| When? | Where? | Description and contact info | Admission |
| Late Mar., Sat. 1-4pm | Wehr Nature Center, 9701 W College Ave, Franklin | Program with short walk to the sugarbush, visit to an old-time sugarin' camp, a boil down demonstration, hands-on activities for children, and a pancake with real maple syrup. http://www.friendsofwehr.org/spring-events/maple-sugar-days/ | $6, free kids <2 |

## CRAFT & RELIC--FRANKLIN (Sp 52/3)

| When? | Where? | Description and contact info | Admission |
|---|---|---|---|
| Mid Apr., Sat., Sun. Sat., Sun. 10am-4pm | Milwaukee County Sports Complex, 6000 Ryan Rd., Franklin | Event with over 150 vendors from across the Midwest, filling their booths with vintage, salvages, industrial, handmade, hand-forged, modern, antiqued, up-cycled, and repurposed goods, including furniture, clothing, garden items, pottery, and more. http://www.recraftandrelic.com/attend.html | $8 and up; free kids <12 |

## MILWAUKEE JOURNAL SENTINEL SPORTS SHOW—WEST ALLIS (Sp 54)

| When? | Where? | Description and contact info | Admission |
|---|---|---|---|
| Early Mar. Sun. thru Wed., see hours on website | State Fair Park Expo Center; 8200 W. Greenfield Ave., West Allis | Exhibits on fishing, hunting, camping, boating and outdoor adventure. www.jssportsshow.com | $7, free kids <13 |

## WINTER POWWOW—WEST ALLIS (Sp 55)

| When? | Where? | Description and contact info | Admission |
|---|---|---|---|
| Mid Mar., Sat. 11am-10pm, Sun. 11am-6pm | State Fair Park Expo Center; 8200 W. Greenfield Ave., West Allis | American Indian traditional powpow with interactive tribal dances planned to include the general public, with extensive marketplace, traditional foods, and family friendly environment. http://wistatefair.com/wsfp/events/ | $8, $6 seniors, free kids <13 |

## WELLNESS, BODY, MIND & SPIRIT EXPO—BROWN DEER (Sp 56)

| When? | Where? | Description and contact info | Admission |
|---|---|---|---|
| Late Apr., Sun. 10am-5pm | Four Points by Sheraton, 8900 North Kildeer Ct., Brown Deer | The latest in new thought presentations, advances in alternative health, and the nation's finest psychics and *mediums*. http://www.wellnessbodymindspirit.com/ | $5 |

## LITTLE WONDERS--FRANKLIN (Sp 57)

| When? | Where? | Description and contact info | Admission |
|---|---|---|---|
| Mar.-May., select Mon.'s 9:30-10:30am 3-year olds; 11-12 3-year olds | Wehr Nature Center, 9701 W College Ave, Franklin | Story, paint with mud (disguised as finger paint), snack, puddle-jumping walk, making mud pies. Register at http://www.friendsofwehr.org/childrens-programs/early-childhood/ | $10 per child (with adult); $7 if Milw. Co. resident |

Bastille Days (Su 118)

Taste of Egypt (Su 165)

Downer Classic Bike Race (Su 61)

Beulah Brinton House (Yr17)

Chill on the Hill (Su 50)

Center Street Days (Su 121)

Doors Open Milwaukee (Fa 22)

Fire Museum (Yr60)

West Allis Farmers' Market    (Su 152) (Fa 100)

Holiday Folk Fair (Fa 88)

Silver City Food and Art Walk (Fa 60)

Summer Soulstice (Su 113)

Milwaukee County Historical Society (Yr13)

Mitchell Park Domes (Yr44);

Musical Mondays (Su 93)

Oktoberfest—West Allis (Fa 30)

River Rhythms (Su 70)

Pet Fest (Fa 80)

Pabst at Doors Open Milwaukee (Fa 22)

Old South Side Settlement Museum (Yr1)

# Rick's picks for the best of 2016

Dragon Boat Festival (Su 107)

Locust Street Festival of Art & Music (Su 124)

Free Ethnic Films by Sokol (Wi 66)

Gay Pride Parade  (Su 64)

# Summer: June, July, August (not in chronological order)

## National Holiday-Specific

## Juneteenth Day

| JUNETEENTH DAY (Su 1) | | | |
|---|---|---|---|
| When? | Where? | Description and contact info | Admission |
| Jun. 19, daytime | Along Martin Luther King Dr. between Center and Burleigh Sts. | Celebration of the US holiday that commemorates the day in 1865 when the end of slavery was announced in Texas, with everything African American—the food, families, music, clothes, dance, exhibits, crafts, art, and a parade. http://juneteenth.com/wisconsin.htm | Free |

## Father's Day

| FATHER & SON HIKE (Su 2) | | | |
|---|---|---|---|
| When? | Where? | Description and contact info | Admission |
| Father's Day weekend, Sat., call for hours | Hawthorn Glen, 1130 N. 60th St. | Hike to explore the wonders of the woods at Hawthorn Glen with campfire to cook hot dogs. 475-5300 | $6 residents (adult must attend with child) |

| MUKWONAGO LIONS SUMMERFESTE (Su 3) | | | |
|---|---|---|---|
| When? | Where? | Description and contact info | Admission |
| Mid Jun., Thu/Fri. 6-11pm, Sat. 8am-11:30pm, Sun. 11am-6:30pm | Field Park, Highways 83 and NN, Mukwonago | Festival of games, amusement rides, food court, fireworks, live music (some may require a cover charge), Father's Day parade, and more. http://www.lakecountryfamilyfun.com/ | Free |

# July 4th

| JULY 4TH CELEBRATION--ALCOTT (Su 4) | | | |
|---|---|---|---|
| **When?** | **Where?** | **Description and contact info** | **Admission** |
| July 4th, all day | Alcott Park, 3751 S. 97th St. | Parade, Doll Buggy, Bike & Trike, and Coaster judging, music, fireworks. http://city.milwaukee.gov/July4th#.V3l_j0QrLIU | Free |

| JULY 4TH CELEBRATION—LAKE PARK (Su 5) | | | |
|---|---|---|---|
| **When?** | **Where?** | **Description and contact info** | **Admission** |
| July 4th, all day | Lake Park, 3233 E. Kenwood Blvd. | Parade, Doll Buggy, Bike & Trike, and Coaster judging, music, fireworks. http://city.milwaukee.gov/July4th#.V3l_j0QrLIU | Free |

| JULY 4TH CELEBRATION—LINCOLN PARK (Su 6) | | | |
|---|---|---|---|
| **When?** | **Where?** | **Description and contact info** | **Admission** |
| July 4th, dusk | Lincoln Park, 1301 W. Hampton Ave. | Fireworks at dusk. http://city.milwaukee.gov/July4th#.V3l_j0QrLIU | Free |

| FIREWORKS AT THE LAKEFRONT (Su 7) | | | |
|---|---|---|---|
| **When?** | **Where?** | **Description and contact info** | **Admission** |
| July 3, dusk (about 9:30) | Lakefront | About 60 minutes of "oohs" and "ahs." http://county.milwaukee.gov/FourthofJuly11324.htm | Free |

| JULY 4TH CELEBRATION--ENDERIS (Su 8) | | | |
|---|---|---|---|
| **When?** | **Where?** | **Description and contact info** | **Admission** |
| July 4, 8:30-11:30am | Enderis Playfield, 2978 N. 72nd | Parade, games, music, watermelon-eating contest. http://city.milwaukee.gov/July4th#.V3l_j0QrLIU | Free |

| JULY 4TH CELEBRATION--GORDON (Su 9) | | | |
|---|---|---|---|
| **When?** | **Where?** | **Description and contact info** | **Admission** |
| July 4, 9am-10pm | Gordon Park, 2828 N. Humboldt Blvd. | Parade, music, kids' activities, art, fireworks. http://city.milwaukee.gov/July4th#.V3l_j0QrLIU | Free |

| JULY 4TH CELEBRATION--HUMBOLDT (Su 10/11) | | | |
|---|---|---|---|
| **When?** | **Where?** | **Description and contact info** | **Admission** |
| July 4, 9am-10pm | Humboldt Park, 3000 S. Howell Ave. | Parade, music, talent show, children's entertainment, fames, fireworks. http://city.milwaukee.gov/July4th#.V3l_j0QrLIU | Free |

| JULY 4TH CELEBRATION--JACKSON (Su 12) | | | |
|---|---|---|---|
| **When?** | **Where?** | **Description and contact info** | **Admission** |
| July 4, 8am-10pm | Jackson Park, 3500 W. Forest Home Ave. | Parade, Doll Buggy, Bike & Trike, and Coaster judging, free ice cream, fireworks. http://city.milwaukee.gov/July4th#.V3l_j0QrLIU | Free |

## JULY 4TH CELEBRATION—MLK (Su 13)

| When? | Where? | Description and contact info | Admission |
|---|---|---|---|
| July 4th, 11:30-12:30am | Dr. M.L. King Center, 1531 W. Vliet St. | Talent show, bike, essay & poetry contest. http://city.milwaukee.gov/July4th#.V3l_j0QrLIU | Free |

## JULY 4TH CELEBRATION--MITCHELL (Su 14)

| When? | Where? | Description and contact info | Admission |
|---|---|---|---|
| July 4th, 9am-10pm | Mitchell Park, 2200 W. Pierce St. | Parade, Doll Buggy, Bike & Trike, and Coaster judging, music, fireworks. http://city.milwaukee.gov/July4th#.V3l_j0QrLIU | Free |

## JULY 4TH CELEBRATION--NOYES (Su 15)

| When? | Where? | Description and contact info | Admission |
|---|---|---|---|
| July 4th, 9am-10pm | Noyes Park, 8235 W. Good Hope Rd. | Parade, Doll Buggy, Bike & Trike, and Coaster judging, games, fireworks. http://city.milwaukee.gov/July4th#.V3l_j0QrLIU | Free |

## JULY 4TH CELEBRATION--SHERMAN (Su 16)

| When? | Where? | Description and contact info | Admission |
|---|---|---|---|
| July 4th, 9am-12:30pm | Sherman Park, 3000 N. Sherman Blvd. | Parade, Doll Buggy, Bike & Trike, and Coaster judging, games. http://city.milwaukee.gov/July4th#.V3l_j0QrLIU | Free |

## JULY 4TH CELEBRATION--WASHINGTON (Su 17)

| When? | Where? | Description and contact info | Admission |
|---|---|---|---|
| July 4th, 11am-10pm | Washington Park, 1859 N. 40th St. | Doll Buggy, Bike & Trike, and Coaster judging, games, fireworks. http://city.milwaukee.gov/July4th#.V3l_j0QrLIU | Free |

## JULY 4TH CELEBRATION--WILSON (Su 18)

| When? | Where? | Description and contact info | Admission |
|---|---|---|---|
| July 4th, 9am-10pm | Wilson Park, 1601 W. Howard Ave. | Parade, Doll Buggy, Bike & Trike, and Coaster judging, music, games, fireworks. http://city.milwaukee.gov/July4th#.V3l_j0QrLIU | Free |

■■■■■■■■■■■■■■■■■■■■■■■■■■■■■■■■■■■■■■■■■■■■■■■■■■■■■■■■■■■

## JULY 4TH CELEBRATION—SOUTH MILWAUKEE (Su 19)

| When? | Where? | Description and contact info | Admission |
|---|---|---|---|
| July 4, 10am-10pm | Grant Park, South Milwaukee | Doll Buggy, Bike & Trike, and Coaster judging, games, music, fireworks. http://smwi.org/celebrations-events/ | Free |

43

## FRANKLIN CIVIC CELEBRATION (Su 20)

| When? | Where? | Description and contact info | Admission |
|-------|--------|------------------------------|-----------|
| Early Jul., Thu. 5-11pm, Fri. 12-11pm, Sat. 12-11pm, Sun. 10am-9:30pm | Lions Legend Park, 9229 W. Loomis Road, Franklin | July 4th celebration with parade, live entertainment, food, artists, fireworks, and more. http://www.franklinwi.gov/Home/Visitors/AnnualCity Events/ FranklinCivicCelebration.htm | Free, but donations welcome |

## JULY 4TH CELEBRATION--CUDAHY (Su 21)

| When? | Where? | Description and contact info | Admission |
|-------|--------|------------------------------|-----------|
| July 4, parade begins at noon | Sheridan Park, 4800 S. Lake Dr., Cudahy | Parade, music, cheer teams. http://www.cudahy-wi.gov/visitors/celebrations_events/index.php | Free |

## JULY 4TH CELEBRATION—ST. FRANCIS (Su 22/23)

| When? | Where? | Description and contact info | Admission |
|-------|--------|------------------------------|-----------|
| July 4, 9:30am-10pm | Oak Leaf Trail, 4800 W. Lake Dr., St. Francis | Parade, Bikes, Trikes, Wagons Contest, games, live music, games, fireworks. https://wi-stfrancis.civicplus.com/ | Free |

## JULY 4TH PARADE--BAYSIDE (Su 24)

| When? | Where? | Description and contact info | Admission |
|-------|--------|------------------------------|-----------|
| July 4, beginning 9am | Bayside Middle School, 601 E. Ellsworth Ln. | Parade that begins at Bayside Middle School and ends at Ellsworth Park. http://www.village.bayside.wi.us/Calendar.aspx? | Free |

## JULY 4TH PARADE—FOX POINT (Su 25)

| When? | Where? | Description and contact info | Admission |
|-------|--------|------------------------------|-----------|
| July 4, beginning 9am | Fox Point Police Dept., 7300 N. Santa Monica Blvd., Fox Point | Parade that starts at the Fox Point Police Department and ends at Longacre Pavilion. https://www.facebook.com/Fox-Point-Police-Department-136459869699142/ | Free |

## JULY 4TH PARADE—WHITEFISH BAY (Su 26)

| When? | Where? | Description and contact info | Admission |
|-------|--------|------------------------------|-----------|
| July 4, beginning 11:30am | N. Kent Ave. and E. Silver Spring Dr., Whitefish Bay | Parade that starts at N. Kent Ave. and E. Silver Spring Drive, and ending at Klode Park; fireworks, 9:30 p.m., Klode Park. http://wfbcivicfoundation.org/ | Free |

## JULY 4TH CELEBRATION--GLENDALE (Su 27)

| When? | Where? | Description and contact info | Admission |
|---|---|---|---|
| July 4, all day | Kletzsch Park, 6560 N. Milwaukee River Pkwy. | Parade, music, fireworks. http://www.glendale-wi.org/ | Free |

## NEW BERLIN 4TH OF JULY FAMILY FESTIVAL (Su 28)

| When? | Where? | Description and contact info | Admission |
|---|---|---|---|
| July 2-4, all day | Malone Park, 16400 W. Al Stigler Parkway, New Berlin | Two days of celebrating with parade, fireworks, pie bake-offs, entertainment, helicopter rides, games. http://www.newberlin.org/index.aspx?nid=671 | Free |

## JULY 4TH PARADE—HALES CORNERS (Su 29)

| When? | Where? | Description and contact info | Admission |
|---|---|---|---|
| July 4, begins 4pm | 102nd and Forest Home Ave., Hales Corners | Independence Day parade, beginning at 102nd & Forest Home Ave. and ending at Village Hall. http://www.halescorners.org/ | Free |

## NAVY BAND GREAT LAKES PERFORMANCE—SOUTH MILWAUKEE (Su 30)

| When? | Where? | Description and contact info | Admission |
|---|---|---|---|
| July 4, 7pm | Grant Park, South Milwaukee | "Fair Winds" and "Brass Ambassadors." https://www.facebook.com/NavyBandGreatLakes/events | Free |

# General

## RENT A BIKE AT VETERANS PARK (Su 31)

| When? | Where? | Description and contact info | Admission |
|---|---|---|---|
| Summer months Sat.'s, Sun.'s, late am to sunset | Veterans Park, 1400 N. Lincoln Memorial Dr. | Bicycle riding along Milwaukee's lakefront. http://www.wheelfunrentals.com/Locations/Milwaukee-2 | $10 adults bikes (cruiser or mountain); $5 kids' bikes |

## KIDS FROM WISCONSIN (Su 32)

| When? | Where? | Description and contact info | Admission |
|---|---|---|---|
| Late Jul., Sun. pm (check website for hours | Marcus Center for the Performing Arts, 929 N. Water St. | Full musical revue for all ages, consisting of 20 singer/dancers and a 13 piece show band performing musical productions to over 100,000 people each summer. http://www.marcuscenter.org/calendar/month/ | Free |

## PECK FLICKS (Su 33)

| When? | Where? | Description and contact info | Admission |
|---|---|---|---|
| Summer months, select Fri's. 7:15pm | Peck Pavilion, Marcus Center for the Performing Arts, 929 N. Water St. | Series offering family friendly movies shown outdoors. http://www.marcuscenter.org/calendar/month/ | Free |

## A.W.E.'S SUMMER TRUCK PROGRAM (Su 34)

| When? | Where? | Description and contact info | Admission |
|---|---|---|---|
| 6 weeks during summer, various weekdays, 12-3pm | Various parks, including Wahl, Gordon, Clarke Sq. and more; see website | Program of meaningful, drop-in, art-based enrichment activities for youth ages 4 – 14, with a focus on working with youth in Milwaukee's under-served neighborhoods. http://county.milwaukee.gov/ParksCalendar | Free |

## WALKING TOUR—RIVER WALK (Su 35)

| When? | Where? | Description and contact info | Admission |
|---|---|---|---|
| Early Jun. thru Aug., Thu.'s 5:30pm | Tour meets in the park at the northwest corner of East St. Paul Ave. and North Water St. | Opportunity to learn about the design concepts used to create the Riverwalk's unique path and enjoy the outdoor sculptures dotting the Riverwalk landscape. http://historicmilwaukee.org/walking-tours/ | $10 adults, $2 kids 7-17, free kids 6 and under |

## WALKING TOUR—HISTORIC THIRD WARD (Su 36)

| When? | Where? | Description and contact info | Admission |
|---|---|---|---|
| Late May thru Aug., Sat.'s, 11am | Meets by the Bublr bike station in front of the Commission House at 400 N. Broadway | Opportunity to learn about the wonderfully designed warehouses and the diverse group of industries that thrived in them in the Third Ward. http://historicmilwaukee.org/walking-tours/ | $10 adults, $2 kids 7-17, free kids 6 and under |

## WALKING TOUR—HISTORIC MILWAUKEE DOWNTOWN (Su 37)

| When? | Where? | Description and contact info | Admission |
|---|---|---|---|
| Late May thru Aug.., 10am | Meets in street level lobby of the Plankinton Building at 161 W. Wisconsin Ave. | Tour that explores the architecture and streetscape to gain insight into how the commercial use of the rivers, lake, and harbor helped create the Milwaukee of today. http://historicmilwaukee.org/walking-tours/ | $10 adults, $2 kids 7-17, free kids 6 and under |

## PICNIC: AFRICANS IN MILWAUKEE (Su 38)

| When? | Where? | Description and contact info | Admission |
|---|---|---|---|
| Late Jul., Sat. 2-9pm | 7835 N Green Bay Ave. | A free celebration of African cultural heritage. http://county.milwaukee.gov/ParksCalendar | Free |

| DAIRY FARM FUN DAY (Su 39) | | | |
|---|---|---|---|
| When? | Where? | Description and contact info | Admission |
| Early Jul., Sat. 9am-2:45pm | Meet bus at MPS Central Services, 5225 W. Vliet, south parking lot door | A visit to Oak Ridge Farm and enjoy hayride, farm animals, dairy farm demonstrations, and picnic campfire (bring own food). Register ahead. 475-8180. | Adult must attend with child, $7 residents |

| RIVERWEST GARDENERS MARKET (Su 40) | | | |
|---|---|---|---|
| When? | Where? | Description and contact info | Admission |
| Mid Jun. thru Aug., Sun. 10am-3pm | Garden Park, 821 E. Locust St., | Fresh produce from Wisconsin farmers, baked goods, arts, crafts. https://riverwestmarket.wordpress.com/ | Free |

| GALLERY NIGHT AND DAY (Su 41) | | | |
|---|---|---|---|
| When? | Where? | Description and contact info | Admission |
| Late Jul., Fri. 5-9pm, Sat. 10am-4pm | Check web page | Milwaukee's two-day premier art event for both the experienced art connoisseur and most beginning admirers that features 50 venues to explore throughout the downtown Milwaukee area four times a year. http://www.historicthirdward.org/events/gallerynight.php | Free |

| ASIA FEST (Su 42) | | | |
|---|---|---|---|
| When? | Where? | Description and contact info | Admission |
| Mid Jun., Fri., Sat., Sun. (early afternoon-evenings) | Veterans Park, 1010 N. Lincoln Memorial Dr. | Interactive performances from various Asian countries. Asian and Asian fusion foods. http://www.asiafestmke.com/ | $10, kids, students, seniors $7 |

| FONDY FARMERS MARKET (Su 43) | | | |
|---|---|---|---|
| When? | Where? | Description and contact info | Admission |
| Jun., Jul., Aug., Sat. 9am-12pm, Tue./Thu. 8am-2pm | 2200 W. Fond du Lac Ave. | Fresh produce from Wisconsin farmers, baked goods, arts, crafts, activities. http://fondymarket.org/ | Free |

| ST. BERNADETTE PARISH FESTIVAL (Su 44) | | | |
|---|---|---|---|
| When? | Where? | Description and contact info | Admission |
| Mid. Jun., Fri. 4:30-11pm, Sat. 12:30-11pm, Sun. 12-7pm | 8200 W. Denver Ave. | Food, raffle, games, carnival rides, bingo, bands. http://www.stbweb.com/our-festival.html | Free |

| BASILICA PARISH PICNIC (Su 45) | | | |
|---|---|---|---|
| When? | Where? | Description and contact info | Admission |
| Late Jun., Sun. 1-5pm | Basilica of St. Josaphat, S. 6th St. & W. Lincoln Ave. | Food, raffles, games, exhibits, look at Basilica.. http://www.thebasilica.org/ | Free |

| ST. PAUL PARISH FESTIVAL (Su 46) | | | |
|---|---|---|---|
| **When?** | **Where?** | **Description and contact info** | **Admission** |
| Late Jun., Thu., Fri., Sat., Sun., see website for hours | 1720 E. Norwich Ave. | Rides, entertainment, food, games, raffle, craft fair, import beer garden. https://www.everfest.com/e/st-paul-parish-festival-milwaukee-wi | Free |

| PELICAN GROVE SWIM (Su 47) | | | |
|---|---|---|---|
| **When?** | **Where?** | **Description and contact info** | **Admission** |
| July, 12:30-4:30 (check website for additional times) | Kosciuszko Park, 2201 S. 7th St. | Outdoor pool with giant- and kid-sized waterslides. http://county.milwaukee.gov/PelicanCove9158.htm | $3, $2 kids 3-11 (must be accompanied by adult) |

| SOUTH SHORE FARMERS MARKET (Su 48) | | | |
|---|---|---|---|
| **When?** | **Where?** | **Description and contact info** | **Admission** |
| Mid Jun. thru Aug, Sat. 8am-12pm | South Shore Park, 2900 South Shore Dr. | Fresh produce from Wisconsin farmers, baked goods, art, crafts, music, demonstrations. https://www.facebook.com/South-Shore-Farmers-Market-352715301468098/ | Free |

| SENIORFEST (Su 49) | | | |
|---|---|---|---|
| **When?** | **Where?** | **Description and contact info** | **Admission** |
| Early Jun., Wed. (check website for hours) | Italian Community Center, 631 E. Chicago St. | Festival of games, food, dancing, music, vendors, for active older adults. http://www.iccmilwaukee.com/main.html | (Check website to access free tickets) |

| CHILL ON THE HILL (Su 50) | | | |
|---|---|---|---|
| **When?** | **Where?** | **Description and contact info** | **Admission** |
| Jun. thru Aug., Tue.'s 6-8pm | Humboldt Park, 3000 S. Howell Ave. | Concerts with name bands, groups; vendors. http://www.bayviewneighborhood.org/chill_on_the_hill | Free |

| SHAKESPEARE IN THREE BRIDGES PARK (Su 51) | | | |
|---|---|---|---|
| **When?** | **Where?** | **Description and contact info** | **Admission** |
| Late Jul., Fri. 7pm | Menomonee Valley behind Palermo Villa next to 33rd Ct. | Play performed by Summit Players along river in the park. http://www.lbwn.org/ | Free, but donations welcome |

| ROLLER SKATING NIGHTS (Su 52) | | | |
|---|---|---|---|
| **When?** | **Where?** | **Description and contact info** | **Admission** |
| Aug., every 3rd Fri. 6-8pm | Our Savior's Lutheran Church, 3022 W. Wisconsin Ave. | Roller skating and skate rentals. www.neighborhoodhousemke.org | Free with 2 non-perishable food items |

### SATURDAY PRE-SCHOOL SERIES (Su 53)

| When? | Where? | Description and contact info | Admission |
|---|---|---|---|
| Jun. thru Aug., select Sat.'s 10:30-11:30am | Riverside Park, 1500 E. Park Pl. | Chance for adults to bring children (ages 3-5) to enjoy nature with indoor or outdoor play. Requires registration. http://urbanecologycenter.org/programs-events-main.html | $7 adults, $5 kids |

### WEDNESDAYS AT THE SHELL IN WASHINGTON PARK (Su 54)

| When? | Where? | Description and contact info | Admission |
|---|---|---|---|
| Summer months, Wed.'s, 6-8:30pm | Washington Park, 1859 N 40th St. | A variety of difference musical genres and bands. http://county.milwaukee.gov/ParksCalendar | Free |

### DOWNTOWN EMPLOYEE APPRECIATION WEEK (Su 55)

| When? | Where? | Description and contact info | Admission |
|---|---|---|---|
| Late Jul., 1 week, 11am-2pm | Zeidler Union Square, 301 W Michigan St | Special events, office challenge games, coffee break in the square, a beach volleyball tournament, lunchtime giveaways and exclusive discounts for downtown Milwaukee's 81,000 employees. http://county.milwaukee.gov/ParksCalendar | Free |

### JACKSON PARK FARMERS MARKET (Su 56)

| When? | Where? | Description and contact info | Admission |
|---|---|---|---|
| Early Jun. thru Aug., Thu. 3:30-7pm | 3300 W. Forest Home Ave. | Fresh food from Wisconsin farms, baked goods, crafts, art. http://jacksonpark.us/farmers-market/ | Free |

### GARDEN DISTRICT ART MARKET (Su 57)

| When? | Where? | Description and contact info | Admission |
|---|---|---|---|
| Late Aug., Sun. 12-4pm | 1 block south of 6th & Howard | Market of artists, food vendors, merchandise vendors, and nonprofit organizations. http://www.milwaukeegdna.com/ | Free |

### BRONZEVILLE JAZZ IN THE HOOD (Su 58)

| When? | Where? | Description and contact info | Admission |
|---|---|---|---|
| Early Jul., Fri. 4-9pm | 4th St. between North and Garfield | Celebration of African-American culture that focuses on local creative entrepreneurial talent with art performances. https://www.facebook.com/events/1717988215085248/ | Free |

### WALKER'S SQUARE FARMERS MARKET (Su 59)

| When? | Where? | Description and contact info | Admission |
|---|---|---|---|
| Mid Jun. thru Aug., Sun., Thu. 8am-5pm | 1031 S. 9th St. | Fresh produce from Wisconsin farmers, baked goods, art, crafts. http://walkersquare.org/farmers-market/ | Free |

| WESTOWN FARMERS MARKET (Su 60) | | | |
|---|---|---|---|
| **When?** | **Where?** | **Description and contact info** | **Admission** |
| Early Jun. thru Aug., Wed. 10am-2pm | Zeidler Union Square, 301 W. Michigan St. | Fresh produce from Wisconsin farmers, baked goods, art, music, crafts. http://westown.org/neighborhood-events/westown-farmers-market/ | Free |

| DOWNER CLASSIC BIKE RACE (Su 61) | | | |
|---|---|---|---|
| **When?** | **Where?** | **Description and contact info** | **Admission** |
| Late Jun., Sat. 10am-8:30pm | Downer Ave. between Bradford and Park. | All day and evening bike races for participants and spectators that are part of the Tour of America's Dairyland Cycling Series, with food, shopping, children's activities. http://murrayhillna.org/events/ | Free (to watch) |

| ST. ROMAN'S FESTIVAL (Su 62) | | | |
|---|---|---|---|
| **When?** | **Where?** | **Description and contact info** | **Admission** |
| Mid Jun., Thu., Fri. 6-11pm; Sat. 2-11pm, Sun. 12-9pm | St. Roman's, 4300 W. 20th St. | Continuous music, rides, prizes, food, http://www.stromans.com/ | Free |

| AUGUST NIGHTS CONCERTS (Su 63) | | | |
|---|---|---|---|
| **When?** | **Where?** | **Description and contact info** | **Admission** |
| Aug., Thu.'s, 6:30-8:30pm | Jackson Park, 3500 W. Forest Home (Picnic Area #2) | Concerts in park. http://county.milwaukee.gov/ParksCalendar | Free |

| GAY PRIDE PARADE (Su 64) | | | |
|---|---|---|---|
| **When?** | **Where?** | **Description and contact info** | **Admission** |
| Mid Jun., Sun. beginning at 2pm | W. 2nd St. from W. Florida to Greenfield | Music and processions celebrating Milwaukee's gay community. http://pridefest.com/ | Free |

| WALKING TOUR—BRADY STREET (Su 65) | | | |
|---|---|---|---|
| **When?** | **Where?** | **Description and contact info** | **Admission** |
| Late May thru Aug., Sat.'s 1:30pm | Meets in front of Three Holy Women Catholic Parish (St. Hedwig Church) at 1702 N. Humboldt Ave. | Tour through the neighborhood on a half-mile stroll and learn about the area's Polish and Italian roots, the counter culture of the '60s and '70s and the area's recent urban renaissance. http://historicmilwaukee.org/walking-tours/ | $10 adults, $2 kids 7-17, free kids 6 and under |

| WALKING TOUR—NORTH POINT MANSIONS (Su 66) | | | |
|---|---|---|---|
| **When?** | **Where?** | **Description and contact info** | **Admission** |
| Check website for dates | Meets at the fountain near the southeast corner of North Ave. and Lake Dr. | Tour of neighborhood that is known for its intact early twentieth century architecture and historical importance. http://historicmilwaukee.org/walking-tours/ | $10 adults, $2 kids 7-17, free kids 6 and under |

## CATHEDRAL SQUARE MARKET (Su 67)

| When? | Where? | Description and contact info | Admission |
|---|---|---|---|
| Early Jun. thru Aug. Sat. 9am-1pm | 520 E. Wells St. | Fresh produce from Wisconsin farms, baked goods, crafts, art, live music, yoga and activities. http://easttown.com/events/cathedral-square-market | Free |

## HARAMBE COMMUNITY MARKET (Su 68)

| When? | Where? | Description and contact info | Admission |
|---|---|---|---|
| Mid Jun. thru Aug., Sat. 12-4pm | Rose Park, 3045 N. MLK Jr. Dr. | Fresh food from Wisconsin farms, baked goods, crafts, art. http://www.hgnimke.org/harambee-community-market | Free |

## NATIONAL LIGHTHOUSE DAY (Su 69)

| When? | Where? | Description and contact info | Admission |
|---|---|---|---|
| Early Aug., Sun. 11-4pm | Northpoint Lighthouse, 2650 N. Wahl Ave. | Opportunity to learn lighthouse history, family activities, climb lighthouse. http://northpointlighthouse.org/events/month/ | $8, $5 seniors & kids 5-11, free kids<4 |

## RIVER RHYTHMS (Su 70)

| When? | Where? | Description and contact info | Admission |
|---|---|---|---|
| Jun. thru Aug, Weds. 6:30-9pm | Pere Marquette Park, 900 N. Plankinton Ave. | Popular bands at riverside location. http://county.milwaukee.gov/Parks | Free |

## ST. ADALBERT PARISH FESTIVAL (Su 71)

| When? | Where? | Description and contact info | Admission |
|---|---|---|---|
| Mid Jun, Fri., 4-10:30pm, Sat., 12-10:30pm, Sun. 1-10:30pm | Parish, 1923 W. Becher St. | Food, mechanical rides, live entertainment. https://www.facebook.com/events/135709666567179/ | $1 |

## FRIENDS OF HANK AARON STATE TRAIL 5K RUN/WALK (Su 72)

| When? | Where? | Description and contact info | Admission |
|---|---|---|---|
| Early Aug., Sat. 7-8:15am | Start and finish near Klement's Sausage Haus (on the east end of Miller Park Stadium) | Opportunity to walk or run in race on Hank Aaron trail, or be a spectator—entertainment and food available. (Requires registration to participate) http://www.hankaaronstatetrail.org/hank-aaron-run-walk.html | Free (to watch) |

## TASTE OF ISLANDS, JAMAICA (Su 73)

| When? | Where? | Description and contact info | Admission |
|---|---|---|---|
| Late Aug., Sat., 2-10pm | Marcus Center Peck Pavilion, 929 N. Water St | Daylong celebration of Jamaica, with hands-on crafts, storytelling, dance, and live music. http://www.marcuscenter.org/ | Free |

## FREE FISHING (Su 74)

| When? | Where? | Description and contact info | Admission |
|---|---|---|---|
| Summer months, anytime | Pond at Kosciuszko Park, 7th-8th along Lincoln Ave. | Fishing experience in well-stocked pond with bait shop 1 block away. (414) 645-4624 | Free |

## WALKING TOUR—BAY VIEW (Su 75)

| When? | Where? | Description and contact info | Admission |
|---|---|---|---|
| Late May thru Aug., Sun.'s 1pm | Meets by the Bublr bike station at Zillman Park, 2180 S Kinnickinnic Ave. | Opportunity to learn the story of how Bay View began with a patchwork of industry and diverse group of immigrants and grew to the charming neighborhood you see today. http://historicmilwaukee.org/walking-tours/ | $10 adults, $2 kids 7-17, free kids 6 and under |

## OPEN ROCK CLIMBING (Su 76)

| When? | Where? | Description and contact info | Admission |
|---|---|---|---|
| Jun.-Sep., 1st Sun. of month 2-4pm | Riverside Park 1500 E. Park Pl. | One free climbing session with the possibility for additional climbs if time allows. http://urbanecologycenter.org/programs-events-main.html | Free, donations welcome |

## TEMPORARY RESURFACING (Su 77)

| When? | Where? | Description and contact info | Admission |
|---|---|---|---|
| Mid Jun., Sat. dusk until midnight | W. Mitchell St. between 9th and 11st St. | Opportunity to watch over 30 artists resurface buildings and other structures on Mitchell Street through video and other visual techniques. http://temporaryresurfacing.org/ | Free |

## HISTORIC MITCHELL SUNFAIR (Su 78)

| When? | Where? | Description and contact info | Admission |
|---|---|---|---|
| Early Jun., Fri. 4-10pm, Sat. 12-10pm, Sun. 12-9pm | W. Mitchell St. between 7th and 11th St. | Street carnival featuring food, beer, vendors, rides, games. http://www.mitchellstreet.com | Free |

## BUCKS SUMMER BLOCK PARTY (Su 79)

| When? | Where? | Description and contact info | Admission |
|---|---|---|---|
| Mid Jun. Sat., 11am-4pm | In front of the Stock-House building on the Schlitz Park campus: on N. 2nd from W. Cherry St. to W, Galena St. (check website as locations sometimes vary) | Opportunity to tip off summer festival season, to enjoy Milwaukee with food, drinks and friends, http://www.nba.com/bucks/ | Free |

## GARDEN DISTRICT FARMERS MARKET (Su 80/81)

| When? | Where? | Description and contact info | Admission |
|---|---|---|---|
| Early Jun.-late Aug., Sat.'s 1-5pm | Just south of Howard on 6th St. | Market of fresh vegetables and other vendors. http://www.milwaukeegdna.com/ | Free |

| MUSIC AND DANCE AT THE PECK (Su 82) | | | |
|---|---|---|---|
| **When?** | **Where?** | **Description and contact info** | **Admission** |
| Summer months, most Tue.'s. times vary | Peck Pavilion, Marcus Center for the Performing Arts, 929 N. Water St. | Local musicians and dance groups providing outdoor entertainment. http://www.marcuscenter.org/calendar/month/ | Free |

| NATIONAL NIGHT OUT—WEDGEWOOD PARK (Su 83) | | | |
|---|---|---|---|
| **When?** | **Where?** | **Description and contact info** | **Admission** |
| First week Aug., weekday 6-8:45pm | Wedgewood Park, 7201 Wedgewood Dr. | Fun evening of free food, games, rides, chance to dialogue with local police and community organizations http://www.safesound.org/events/national-night-out-events-across-milwaukee/ | Free |

| POETRY IN THE PARK (Su 84) | | | |
|---|---|---|---|
| **When?** | **Where?** | **Description and contact info** | **Admission** |
| Aug., select Tue.'s, 6:30-8pm (check website) | Juneau Park, Prospect Ave. & Kilbourn Ave., near Juneau statue | Poetry readings by known poets. https://www.facebook.com/Juneau-Park-Friends-113584992257/ | Free |

| POLISH FEST FRIDAY PROMOTION (Su 85) | | | |
|---|---|---|---|
| **When?** | **Where?** | **Description and contact info** | **Admission** |
| Mid Jun., Fri.-Sat., 12pm-12am, Sun. 12-8pm | 639 E. Summerfest Pl. | Celebration of Polish traditions, music, food, music, kids' activities. http://www.polishfest.org/ | 50 cents on Fri. 12-5pm |

| POLISH FEST SATURDAY PROMOTION (Su 86) | | | |
|---|---|---|---|
| **When?** | **Where?** | **Description and contact info** | **Admission** |
| Mid Jun., Fri.-Sat., 12pm-12am, Sun. 12pm-8pm | 639 E. Summerfest Pl. | Celebration of Polish traditions, music, food, music, kids' activities. http://www.polishfest.org/ | Free on Sat. 8pm-12am with 3 or more non-perishable food items |

| URBAN STARGAZING (Su 87) | | | |
|---|---|---|---|
| **When?** | **Where?** | **Description and contact info** | **Admission** |
| Early Jun., Thu.'s 7-8:30pm | Riverside Park, 1500 E. Park Pl. | Lively discussion about astronomy and if the skies are clear, might go stargazing. http://urbanecologycenter.org/programs-events-main.html | Free, but $5 donation suggested |

| LAKEFRONT MOVIES (Su 88) | | | |
|---|---|---|---|
| **When?** | **Where?** | **Description and contact info** | **Admission** |
| Mid Jun. to early Sept., see website | Veterans Park, 1010 N. Lincoln Memorial Dr. | Blockbuster family films shown in beautiful setting (food and beverages available for purchase from the Gift of Wings Kite Store). http://county.milwaukee.gov/FamilyFlicks21477.htm | Free |

| SUMMER ON OLYMPUS: SUMMER FLORAL SHOW (Su 89) | | | |
|---|---|---|---|
| **When?** | **Where?** | **Description and contact info** | **Admission** |
| Mid Jun.-mid Sep., Mon.'s 9am-4pm | Mitchell Park Domes, 524 S Layton Blvd. | Opportunity to see the best in summer blooms. http://county.milwaukee.gov/ParksCalendar | Free on Mondays |

| ST. ROMAN'S ANNUAL FESTIVAL (Su 90) | | | |
|---|---|---|---|
| **When?** | **Where?** | **Description and contact info** | **Admission** |
| Mid Jun., Thu. 6-11pm, Fri. 6-11pm, Sat. 2-11pm, Sun. 12-9pm | 1710 W. Bolivar Ave. | Festival of continuous music, food, rides, raffle, other cash prizes, and more. http://www.stromans.com/ | Free |

| ARMENIAN FEST (Su 91) | | | |
|---|---|---|---|
| **When?** | **Where?** | **Description and contact info** | **Admission** |
| Late Jul., Sun. 11am-6pm | St. John the Baptist Armenian Orthodox Church, 7825 W. Layton Ave. | Festival of Armenian food, dancing, cultural booths, and more. http://www.armenianfest.com/ | Free |

| MUSICAL MONDAYS (Su 93) | | | |
|---|---|---|---|
| **When?** | **Where?** | **Description and contact info** | **Admission** |
| Mid Jul.-late Aug., Mon.'s 6:30-8pm | 2975 N. Lake Park Rd. | Varied roster of musicians perform. http://lakeparkfriends.org/visit/events/music-in-the-park/ | Free |

| LAKEFRONT FESTIVAL OF THE ARTS (Su 94) | | | |
|---|---|---|---|
| **When?** | **Where?** | **Description and contact info** | **Admission** |
| Mid Jun., Fri. 10am-10pm, Sat., 10am-7pm, Sun. 10am-5pm | Milwaukee Art Museum, 700 N. Art Museum Dr. | Exhibits of over 170 different artists with food and entertainment. http://lfoa.mam.org/event-info | $10 if purchased in advance |

## WONDERFUL WEDNESDAYS (Su 95)

| When? | Where? | Description and contact info | Admission |
|---|---|---|---|
| Early Jul.-mid Aug., Wed.'s, 6:30-7:30pm | Lake Park, 2975 N Lake Park Rd. | Concerts for kids and families. http://county.milwaukee.gov/ParksCalendar | Free |

## FONDY'S FARMERS MARKET—SCHLITZ PARK (Su 96)

| When? | Where? | Description and contact info | Admission |
|---|---|---|---|
| Late Jun. thru Aug. (see website for hours) | Schlitz Park | Fresh produce from Wisconsin farmers, baked goods, art, music, crafts. http://fondymarket.org | |

## HOT RODS-N-BLUES CAR SHOW--GRAFTON (Su 97)

| When? | Where? | Description and contact info | Admission |
|---|---|---|---|
| Late Jun., Sun. 9am-3:30pm | Lime Kiln Park, Grafton | Car, truck, motorcycle show and blues music. https://www.facebook.com/Hot-Rods-N-Blues-101929409845444/ | Free |

## RHYTHM & BLOOM CONCERT SERIES (Su 98)

| When? | Where? | Description and contact info | Admission |
|---|---|---|---|
| Late Jul.to mid Aug., Thu.'s, 6-8:30pm | Green Tree Community Garden, 60th & Green Tree Rd. | Concerts with a variety of bands, food, food trucks. http://havenwoods.org/rhythm-blooms-concert-series/ | Free |

## SECRET GARDEN (Su 99)

| When? | Where? | Description and contact info | Admission |
|---|---|---|---|
| Warm weather months, Mon.-Wed. 12-8pm, Thu., Fri. 10am-6pm, Sat. 10am-5pm | Tippecanoe Library, 3912 S. Howell Ave. | An outdoor space for children and the telling of stories inspired by the Frances Hodgson Burnett's 1911 book, *The Secret Garden*. http://www.mpl.org/hours_locations/tippecanoe.php | Free |

## FESTA ITALIANA (Su 100)

| When? | Where? | Description and contact info | Admission |
|---|---|---|---|
| Late Jul., Fri. –Sat. 11:30am-12am, Sun. 11:30am-11pm | 639 E. Summerfest Pl. | Celebration of Italian traditions, music, food, music, kids' activities. http://festaitaliana.com/tickets/ | $10 if ticket is purchased in advance |

## IRISH FEST FRIDAY PROMOTION (Su 101)

| When? | Where? | Description and contact info | Admission |
|---|---|---|---|
| Mid. Aug., Thu. 5-10pm, Fri. 4pm-12am, Sat., 12pm-12am, Sun. 11am-10pm | 639 E. Summerfest Pl. | Celebration of Irish traditions, music, food, music, kids' activities. http://irishfest.com/Irishfest.htm | $10 Fri. only |

## GERMAN FEST FRIDAY PROMOTION (Su 102)

| When? | Where? | Description and contact info | Admission |
|---|---|---|---|
| Late Jul., Fri. 3pm-12am, Sat. 12pm-12am, Sun. 12pm-9pm | 639 E. Summerfest Pl. | Celebration of German traditions, music, food, music, kids' activities. http://germanfest.com/ | $3 Fri. only |

## US AIR FORCE BAND OF MID-AMERICA CONCERT (Su 103)

| When? | Where? | Description and contact info | Admission |
|---|---|---|---|
| Summer, see website | Marcus Center for the Arts, Uihlein Hall, 929 N Water St. | Concert tour of largest ensemble in the Air National Guard Band that includes stops in Milwaukee. http://www.marcuscenter.org/calendar/month/ | Free |

## NATIONAL NIGHT OUT—NEAR WEST SIDE (Su 104)

| When? | Where? | Description and contact info | Admission |
|---|---|---|---|
| First week Aug., weekday 2-6pm | Near West Side: West Side Market, 1201 N. 35th St. | Fun evening of free food, games, rides, chance to dialogue with local police and community organizations, http://www.safesound.org/events/national-night-out-events-across-milwaukee/ | Free |

## STARS & S'MORES (Su 105)

| When? | Where? | Description and contact info | Admission |
|---|---|---|---|
| Late Aug., Wed. 7-8:30pm | Manfred Olson Planetarium, UW-M Physics building, 1900 E. Kenwood Blvd. | Opportunity to make delicious s'mores with friends and family while looking through telescopes and enjoying a special Planetarium program as well! http://uwm.edu/planetarium/shows/special-events/ | $3 |

## TIE-DYING SHIRTS (Su 106)

| When? | Where? | Description and contact info | Admission |
|---|---|---|---|
| Late Aug., Wed. 5-7pm | Manfred Olson Planetarium, UW-M Physics building, 1900 E. Kenwood Blvd. | Chance to make a tie-dyed T-shirt and get a free s'mores kit with each shirt. http://uwm.edu/planetarium/shows/special-events/ | $10 |

## MILWAUKEE DRAGON BOAT FESTIVAL (Su 107)

| When? | Where? | Description and contact info | Admission |
|---|---|---|---|
| Late Jul. Sat. 8am-5pm | Veterans Park, 1010 N Lincoln Memorial Dr | A showcase of Chinese culture, traditions, games, boat races, food. http://www.milwaukeedragonboatfest.org/ | Free |

## INDIAFEST (Su 108)

| When? | Where? | Description and contact info | Admission |
|---|---|---|---|
| Mid Aug., Sat., 11am-9pm | Humboldt Park, 3000 S. Howell Ave. | Celebration of Indian culture, including music and dance performances, a fashion show, singing competition, authentic Indian cuisine and marketplace. http://www.indiafestmilwaukee.org/ | Free |

## WISCONSIN LUTHERAN ART & CRAFT FAIR (Su 109)

| When? | Where? | Description and contact info | Admission |
|---|---|---|---|
| Early Jul., Sat. 9am-4pm | Wisconsin Lutheran College campus, 8800 W. Bluemound Rd. | Arts & crafts booths, silent auction, music, food. http://www.wlc.edu/ | Free |

## BRADY ST. FESTIVAL (Su 110)

| When? | Where? | Description and contact info | Admission |
|---|---|---|---|
| Late Jul., Sat. 11am-12am | Brady St. | Music, food, arts, crafts. http://bradystreet.org/documents/20-brady-st-festival- | Free |

## ST. MATTHIAS PARISH FESTIVAL (Su 111)

| When? | Where? | Description and contact info | Admission |
|---|---|---|---|
| Late Aug., Fri. 5-11pm, Sat. 2-11pm, Sun. 12-8pm | 92nd & Oklahoma Ave. | Fish fries, chicken dinners, raffles, bands, vendors. http://www.stmatthias-milw.org/ | Free |

## FREE MEXICAN FIESTA (Su 112)

| When? | Where? | Description and contact info | Admission |
|---|---|---|---|
| Late Aug., Fri. 12pm-12am, Sat. 12pm-12am, Sun. 12pm-9pm | 639 E. Summerfest Pl. | Celebration of Mexican traditions, music, food, music, kids' activities. http://mexicanfiesta.org/mexican_fiesta.php | Free tickets Fri. 12-3pm |

## SUMMER SOULSTICE MUSIC FEST (Su 113)

| When? | Where? | Description and contact info | Admission |
|---|---|---|---|
| Late Jun., Sat. 10am-12pm | East end of North Ave. | Largest showcase of top music acts in the region, with visual artists, arts fair, creation stations, chefs, stunt bikes, and family-friendly activities. http://www.theeastside.org/happenings/summer-soulstice | Free |

## MORNING GLORY FINE CRAFT FAIR (Su 114)

| When? | Where? | Description and contact info | Admission |
|---|---|---|---|
| Mid Aug., Sat. & Sun. (see website for times) | Marcus Center for the Performing Arts, 929 N. Water St. | Fair featuring over 100 fine craft artists exhibiting ceramics, glass, leather, wood, photography, jewelry, fiber, enamel, handmade paper, metal, and mixed. media. http://www.wdcc.org/ | Free |

## NATIONAL NIGHT OUT--SOUTH SIDE (Su 115)

| When? | Where? | Description and contact info | Admission |
|---|---|---|---|
| First week Aug., weekday 4-8pm | Kosciuszko Park, 2201 S. 7th St. | Fun evening of free food, games, rides, chance to dialogue with local police and community organizations, http://www.safesound.org/events/national-night-out-events-across-milwaukee/ | Free |

| PADDLE BOAT RENTALS (Su 116) | | | |
|---|---|---|---|
| When? | Where? | Description and contact info | Admission |
| Summer months, daily 10am-7pm, weather permitting | Juneau Park, 801 N. Lincoln Memorial Dr. | Paddle boating with views of Milwaukee skyline and Lake Michigan. http://juneauparkpaddleboats.com/fleet.html | $5 per person per half hour, if < 16 need parental consent |

| SAIL BOAT RENTALS (Su 117) | | | |
|---|---|---|---|
| When? | Where? | Description and contact info | Admission |
| Summer months., daily 10am-7pm, weather permitting | Juneau Park, 801 N. Lincoln Memorial Dr. | Sail boating with views of Milwaukee skyline and Lake Michigan. http://juneauparkpaddleboats.com/fleet.html | $5 per boat per half hour, if < 16 need parental consent |

| BASTILLE DAYS (Su 118) | | | |
|---|---|---|---|
| When? | Where? | Description and contact info | Admission |
| Mid Jul., Thu. thru Sun. (see website for hours) | Cathedral Square Park 520 E. Wells St. | French festival with live music, international marketplace, French and Cajun cuisine. www.easttown.com/events/bastille-days/ | Free |

| BRONZEVILLE WEEK (Su 119) | | | |
|---|---|---|---|
| When? | Where? | Description and contact info | Admission |
| Aug., 2nd week | MLK Dr., between Garfield Ave. and Center St. | Cultural and arts festival, with a run/walk event, health screenings, trolley rides, arts night, poetry readings. mcoggs@milwaukee.gov | Free |

| NATIONAL NIGHT OUT—NORTHWEST SIDE (Su 120) | | | |
|---|---|---|---|
| When? | Where? | Description and contact info | Admission |
| First week Aug., weekday 5:30-8:30pm | Kops Park: 3321 N. 86th St. | Fun evening of free food, games, rides, chance to dialogue with local police and community organizations, http://www.safesound.org/events/national-night-out-events-across-milwaukee/ | Free |

| CENTER STREET DAYS (Su 121) | | | |
|---|---|---|---|
| When? | Where? | Description and contact info | Admission |
| Early Aug., Sat. all day | Center St. between Humboldt Ave. & Holton St. | Music, food, arts, crafts, cart race, car show. http://www.centerstreetdazefestival.com/ | Free |

| NATIONAL NIGHT OUT—NORTH SIDE (Su 122) | | | |
|---|---|---|---|
| When? | Where? | Description and contact info | Admission |
| First week Aug., weekday 4-8pm | Lincoln Park: 1301 W. Hampton Ave. | Fun evening of free food, games, rides, chance to dialogue with local police and community organizations, http://www.safesound.org/events/national-night-out-events-across-milwaukee/ | Free |

## SUMMER EVENINGS OF MUSIC (Su 123)

| When? | Where? | Description and contact info | Admission |
|---|---|---|---|
| Beginning mid Jun., approx. weekly for summer (see website), 7:30-9pm | Helene Zelazo Center for the Performing Arts, 2419 E. Kenwood Blvd. | Fine arts quartet and others; RSVP https://www4.uwm.edu/psoa/fineartsquartet | $10 |

## LOCUST STREET FESTIVAL OF MUSIC AND ART (Su 124/25)

| When? | Where? | Description and contact info | Admission |
|---|---|---|---|
| Mid Jun., Sun. 11am-8pm | Locust St. between Humboldt & Holton | Festival featuring six live music venues and a variety of food, artists and vendors with up to 30,000 people. https://www.facebook.com/Locust-Street-Festival-of-Music-and-Art-119283148109243/ | Free |

## JAZZ IN THE PARK (Su 126)

| When? | Where? | Description and contact info | Admission |
|---|---|---|---|
| Jun., Thu.'s 5-9pm | Cathedral Square Park, Kilbourn Ave. & N. Jefferson St. | An outdoor music tradition in Milwaukee featuring an eclectic lineup of jazz, big band, funk, R & B, reggae, blues and more. http://easttown.com/events/jazz-in-the-park | Free |

## LIVE AT THE LAKE (Su 127)

| When? | Where? | Description and contact info | Admission |
|---|---|---|---|
| Jul., Mon.'s 6:30-8pm | Lake Park, 3233 E. Kenwood Blvd. | The East Side's offering to free outdoor music, set in one of Milwaukee's most treasured parks. http://www.liveatthelakefront.com/ | Free |

## WALKING TOUR—BAY VIEW (Su 128)

| When? | Where? | Description and contact info | Admission |
|---|---|---|---|
| Late May-late Aug. Sun.'s 1pm | Meets by the Bublr bike station at Zillman Park, 2180 S Kinnickinnic Ave. | Opportunity to learn the story of how Bay View began with a patchwork of industry and diverse group of immigrants and grew to the charming neighborhood you see today. http://historicmilwaukee.org/walking-tours/ | $10 adults, $2 kids 7-17, free kids 6 and under |

## COMMUNITY UNITY DAY BLOCK PARTY (Su 129)

| When? | Where? | Description and contact info | Admission |
|---|---|---|---|
| Aug., see contact info | Garden Park, 2819 W. Richardson Pl. | Block party for residents and central city churches, featuring vendors and performers. contact Claire Van Fossen, (414) 933 6161, or https://www.neighborhoodhousemke.org/news/community-unity-day/ | Free |

## WORLD REFUGEE DAY (Su 130)

| When? | Where? | Description and contact info | Admission |
|---|---|---|---|
| June, annually, see website | Milwaukee parks; varies | Refugee groups participate in cultural performances and games such as soccer. www.facebook.com/MilwaukeeWorldRefugeeDay | Free |

## SKYLINE MUSIC SERIES (Su 131)

| When? | Where? | Description and contact info | Admission |
|---|---|---|---|
| Early Jul. thru late Aug., Tue.'s 5:30 | Kadish Park, south of North Ave., west of Bremen St. | A great evening of music in Riverwest, topped off with one of the most dramatic views of the city. http://www.coa-yfc.org/wp/skyline/ | Free |

## AYRE IN THE SQUARE (Su 132)

| When? | Where? | Description and contact info | Admission |
|---|---|---|---|
| Mid Jun. thru late Aug., Thu.'s 6:30-8:30 | Catalano Square, at Broadway and Menomonee St. | An evening series featuring an eclectic mix of local artists. http://musicinthesquare.org/site/ | Free |

## PUERTO RICAN FEST (Su 133)

| When? | Where? | Description and contact info | Admission |
|---|---|---|---|
| Midsummer, annually | Varies | Puerto Rican bands, a car show, motorcycle exhibits, and traditional Puerto Rican food— including roasted pig. www.conquistadornews.com/. | Free |

## SUMMERFEST FOR FREE (Su 134)

| When? | Where? | Description and contact info | Admission |
|---|---|---|---|
| Late Jun., opening day, 12-3pm | 639 E. Summerfest Pl. | World's largest music festival, with food, drinks, activities for all. http://summerfest.com/ | Free with 3 nonperishable food items |

## SOUTH SHORE FROLICS (Su 135)

| When? | Where? | Description and contact info | Admission |
|---|---|---|---|
| Mid Jul., Fri. 4-10:30pm, Sat. 12-10:30pm, Sun. 9am-10pm | 2900 South Shore Dr. | Fireworks, bands, food, games, classic cars, art show, drinks. http://www.southshorefrolics.org/ | Free |

| KASHUBIAN PICNIC (Su 136) | | | |
| --- | --- | --- | --- |
| When? | Where? | Description and contact info | Admission |
| First Saturday in August, see website for hours | Kaszub Park on Jones Island | Picnic sponsored by descendants of former settlers on Jones Island with music, food, cultural presentations. https://www.facebook.com/HistoricalPlace | Free |

∎∎∎∎∎∎∎∎∎∎∎∎∎∎∎∎∎∎∎∎∎∎∎∎∎∎∎∎∎∎∎∎∎∎∎∎∎∎∎∎∎∎∎∎∎∎∎∎∎∎∎

| OZAUKEE COUNTY FAIR--CEDARBURG (Su 137) | | | |
| --- | --- | --- | --- |
| When? | Where? | Description and contact info | Admission |
| Early Aug., Tue. thru Sun., (hours vary) | Fair grounds at W67 N866 Washington Ave., Cedarburg | Midway, livestock, youth pavilion, horse show, truck/tractor pull, crafts, nutrition, live entertainment, exhibits, food. http://www.ozaukeecountyfair.com/ | Free |

| MUSIC ON MAIN—WEST BEND (Su 138) | | | |
| --- | --- | --- | --- |
| When? | Where? | Description and contact info | Admission |
| Early Jun. thru early Sep., Thu.'s 6:30-9:30pm | Old Settlers Park, 6th Ave. & Main St., West Bend | Summer Concert Series in Old Settler's Park. http://www.downtownwestbend.com/music-onoff-main.html | Free |

| SUMMER SOUNDS IN CEDARBURG (Su 139) | | | |
| --- | --- | --- | --- |
| When? | Where? | Description and contact info | Admission |
| Jun. thru Aug., Fri.'s. 6:30-10pm | Cedar Creek Park, W62 N590 Washington Avenue, Cedarburg | Music, food and fun at the park. http://www.summersounds.net/ | Free |

| BROOKFIELD FARMERS MARKET (Su 140) | | | |
| --- | --- | --- | --- |
| When? | Where? | Description and contact info | Admission |
| Jun. thru Aug., Sat. 7:30am-12pm | 2000 N. Calhoun Rd. | Fresh produce from Wisconsin farmers; arts/crafts fair every third Sun. of month. http://www.brookfieldfarmersmarket.com/ | Free |

| KRAUT MUSIC FEST--FRANKSVILLE (Su 141) | | | |
| --- | --- | --- | --- |
| When? | Where? | Description and contact info | Admission |
| Mid Jun., Thu.5-10pm, Fri. 12-11pm, Sat. 11am-11pm, Sun. 11am-8pm | Caledonian Pleasant Memorial Park, Franksville | Festival of live music, Kraut king and queen competition, food, beverages, and midway carnival rides. https://krautmusicfest.com/ | $10 |

| PEWAUKEE KIWANIS BEACH PARTY (Su 142) | | | |
| --- | --- | --- | --- |
| When? | Where? | Description and contact info | Admission |
| Late Jun., Fri. 8am-11pm, Sat. 7am-11pm | Lakefront Park, 222 W. Wisconsin Ave., Pewaukee | Party of food, live music, beverages, games, and performances by the Pewaukee ski club. http://www.pewaukeekiwanis.org/beach-party | Free |

## GREECIAN FEST AT SAINTS CONSTANTINE AND HELEN CHURCH--WAUWATOSA (Su 143)

| When? | Where? | Description and contact info | Admission |
|---|---|---|---|
| Mid Jun. Fri. 4-10pm, Sat., 12-10pm, Sun. 12-10pm | 2160 N. Wauwatosa Ave, Wauwatosa | Festival of Greek food, dance, music, marketplace, children's games. http://www.stsconstantinehelenwi.org/grecian-fest/ | Free |

## WEDNESDAY NIGHT THUNDER—WEST ALLIS (Su 144)

| When? | Where? | Description and contact info | Admission |
|---|---|---|---|
| Mid Jul., Wed.'s, 2:30pm-sunset | Milwaukee Mile, 640 S. 84th St., West Allis | High performance driving sessions on the Milwaukee Mile Road Course (non-competitive). http://www.milwaukeetrackdays.com | Free to spectators |

## WEDNESDAY NIGHT LIVE—WEST ALLIS (Su 145)

| When? | Where? | Description and contact info | Admission |
|---|---|---|---|
| Jun., Jul., Aug. Wed.'s, 6-11pm | State Fair Park, Budweiser Pavilion, 640 S. 84th St., West Allis | Milwaukee's most popular local bands entertain thousands of fans each week at this indoor/outdoor family friendly concert venue. http://budpavilion.com | Free |

## TRIMBORN FARM--GREENDALE (Su 146)

| When? | Where? | Description and contact info | Admission |
|---|---|---|---|
| May 15 thru Aug., 10am-10pm; by appointment | 8881 W. Grange Ave., Greendale, WI | A guided tour of the only Milwaukee County park with a historic theme. Call 414-273-8288 to reserve a tour. http://www.milwaukeehistory.net/historic-sites-2/trimborn-farm/ | $5 for tour, kids < 6 free |

## FIREFLY ART FAIR--WAUWATOSA (Su 147)

| When? | Where? | Description and contact info | Admission |
|---|---|---|---|
| Early Aug., Sat., Sun. 10am-4pm | Kneeland Walker House, 7406 Hillcrest Dr., Wauwatosa | Over 90 juried artists exhibiting their crafts, representing an eclectic array of art from a variety of media. http://wauwatosahistoricalsociety.org/ | Free |

## GREEK FEST—WEST ALLIS (Su 148)

| When? | Where? | Description and contact info | Admission |
|---|---|---|---|
| Late Jun. Fri./Sat. 11am-11pm, Sun. 11am-9pm | State Fair Park, 640 S. 84th St., West Allis | Festival of Greek food, dance, concerts, marketplace. https://www.facebook.com/MkeGreekFest | Free |

## AMERICAN ACCENTS FESTIVAL OF FINE ARTS & CRAFTS--HARTFORD (Su 149)

| When? | Where? | Description and contact info | Admission |
|---|---|---|---|
| Mid Aug., Sat. 9am-3pm | Willowbrook Park, 774 E. Sumner St., Hartford | Festival featuring over 80 craftsmen and artisans offering all handmade items, with music. http://www.hartfordwomensclub.org/craftfairs.html | Free |

| ART IN THE PARK—MENOMONEE FALLS (Su 150) | | | |
|---|---|---|---|
| **When?** | **Where?** | **Description and contact info** | **Admission** |
| Late Aug., Sun. 10am-4pm | Mill Pond Park, Main St., Menomonee Falls | Event to showcase the art (amateur and professional) of Menomonee Falls artists. http://artguildmf.org/ | Free |

| ART, CRAFTS & FARM MARKET SHOW--HUBERTUS (Su 151) | | | |
|---|---|---|---|
| **When?** | **Where?** | **Description and contact info** | **Admission** |
| Early Jun., Sat. and Sun., see website for hours | Holy Hill Art Farm, 4958 Highway 167, Hubertus | Art show at 70-acre farm in Kettle Moraine, featuring a selected blend of fine art, crafts, vintage & antiques. http://www.holyhillartfarm.com/ | Free |

| TOSA FARMERS MARKET (Su 152) | | | |
|---|---|---|---|
| **When?** | **Where?** | **Description and contact info** | **Admission** |
| Jun. thru Aug., Sat. 8am-12pm | 7720 Harwood Ave., Wauwatosa | Fresh produce from Wisconsin farmers, baked goods, arts, crafts. http://tosafarmersmarket.com/ | Free |

| CONCERT IN THE PARK—HALES CORNERS (Su 153) | | | |
|---|---|---|---|
| **When?** | **Where?** | **Description and contact info** | **Admission** |
| Summer months, Thu.'s 6:30pm | Boerner Botanical Gardens, 9400 Boerner Dr., Hales Corner | A mixture of musical genres with opportunity to purchase snacks and enjoy garden. http://county.milwaukee.gov/ParksCalendar | Free |

| WEST BEND GERMANFEST (Su 154) | | | |
|---|---|---|---|
| **When?** | **Where?** | **Description and contact info** | **Admission** |
| Late Aug., Thu. 5-11pm, Fri. 2-11pm, Sat. 2-11pm, Sun. 12-7pm | Main and Walnut St., downtown West Bend | Festival of German food, live music, games, Sheepshead tournament, and more. http://westbendgermanfest.com/ | Free |

| WEST ALLIS FARMERS MARKET (Su 155) | | | |
|---|---|---|---|
| **When?** | **Where?** | **Description and contact info** | **Admission** |
| Jun. thru Aug., Tue. 12-6pm, Sat. 1-6pm | 6501 W. National Ave. | Fresh produce from Wisconsin farmers; baked goods, arts, crafts. https://www.facebook.com/westallisfarmersmarket/ | Free |

| CROATIANFEST--FRANKLIN (Su 156) | | | |
|---|---|---|---|
| **When?** | **Where?** | **Description and contact info** | **Admission** |
| Mid Jul., Sat. 11am-11pm; Sun. 11am-6pm | Croatian Park, 9100 S. 76th St., Franklin | Festival with Croatian food, live music, kids' activities, games, and more. http://milwaukeecroatians.org/croatian-park/croatian-fest/ | $5, free, free for all on Sun. |

| SHOREWOOD FARMERS MARKET (Su 157) | | | |
|---|---|---|---|
| **When?** | **Where?** | **Description and contact info** | **Admission** |
| Mid Jun. thru Aug., Sun. 9:30am-1pm | Lake Bluff Elementary, 1600 W. Bluff Blvd.Shorewood | Fresh produce from Wisconsin farmers, baked goods, live entertainment, family events, arts, crafts. http://www.shorewoodfarmersmarket.com/ | Free |

| EAA AIRVENTURE--OSHKOSH (Su 158/159) | | | |
|---|---|---|---|
| **When?** | **Where?** | **Description and contact info** | **Admission** |
| Late Jul., one week (check website for schedule) | Wittman Regional Airport, Oshkosh | The world's greatest aviation celebration with Warbirds. Vintage, Homebuilts, Ultralights, Aerobatics. http://www.eaa.org/en/airventure | Free |

| ST. MARY'S FAMILY FUN FESTIVAL--WAUKESHA (Su 160) | | | |
|---|---|---|---|
| **When?** | **Where?** | **Description and contact info** | **Admission** |
| Late June, Fri., 5-11pm, Sat. 4-11pm, Sun. 12-6pm | 225 S. Hartwell Ave, Waukesha | Large festival of games, food, vendors, rides, raffle, bingo tent , beer tent, fireworks, and more https://www.facebook.com/StMaryWaukeshaFamily FunFestival | Free |

| AGATE EXPO--CEDARBURG (Su 161) | | | |
|---|---|---|---|
| **When?** | **Where?** | **Description and contact info** | **Admission** |
| Early Jul., Thu. through Sun. | Cedarburg High School W68 N611 Evergreen Blvd., Cedarburg | Expo includes collections, educational stories, sale of all things silica, vendors, exhibits, and a symposium of worldwide agate experts. http://www.cedarburg.org/event/2734475-2016-agate-expo-in-cedarburg-wi | Free |

| KETTLE MORAINE DAYS--EAGLE (Su 162) | | | |
|---|---|---|---|
| **When?** | **Where?** | **Description and contact info** | **Admission** |
| Late Jun., Fri., Sat., Sun. | Eagle Village Park, 401 Markham Road, Eagle | Weekend of live music, talent show, food, free kids' activities, raffle, parade, games. http://www.kettlemorainedays.com/ | Free |

| SUSSEX LIONS DAZE (Su 163) | | | |
|---|---|---|---|
| **When?** | **Where?** | **Description and contact info** | **Admission** |
| Mid Jul., Fri. 6pm-12am; Sat. 8:30am-12am, Sun. 10:30am-7pm | Sussex Village Park, N64-W23760 Main St., Sussex | Festival of carnival rides, fireworks, food, live entertainment, softball tournament, tractor pull, bingo, and more. http://www.sussexlions.org/lionsdaze/index.htm | Free |

| ELIZABETH ANN SETON FUNFEST—NEW BERLIN (Su 164) | | | |
|---|---|---|---|
| **When?** | **Where?** | **Description and contact info** | **Admission** |
| Late Jul., Fri. 7-11pm, Sat. 7-11pm, Sun. 12-5:30pm | 12700 W. Howard Ave., New Berlin | Festival of live entertainment, games, inflatable rides, raffle, bake sale, bingo. http://www.mystelizabeth.com/parish-life/funfest/ | Free |

| TASTE OF EGYPT—OAK CREEK (Su 165) | | | |
|---|---|---|---|
| When? | Where? | Description and contact info | Admission |
| Late Aug., Fri. 12-8pm, Sat. 10am-80pm, Sun. 11am-7pm | St. Mary and St. Antonious Coptic Orthodox Church, 1521 W. Drexel Ave., Oak Creek | Opportunity to sample Egyptian foods at Egyptian Christian church, alcohol-free family fun. https://www.facebook.com/tasteofegyptmke | Free |

| HARTLAND'S HOMETOWN CELEBRATION--HARTLAND (Su 166) | | | |
|---|---|---|---|
| When? | Where? | Description and contact info | Admission |
| Late Jun., Fri. 5-11pm, Sat. 12-11pm, Sun. 1-4pm | Nixon Park, 175 E. Park Ave., Hartland | Festival of live music, talent contest, arts & crafts vendors, food, parade on Sunday. http://www.downtownhartland.com/hartland-hometown-celebration/ | Free |

| GREENDALE LIONS CLUB VILLAGE DAYS (Su 167) | | | |
|---|---|---|---|
| When? | Where? | Description and contact info | Admission |
| Mid Aug., Fri., Sat., Sun. (see website for hours) | 5600 Parking St., Greendale. | Celebration with food, live music, games, raffle, and rummage sale. http://www.greendalelions.org/villagedays.html | Free |

| ST. RITA PARISH FESTIVAL—WEST ALLIS (Su 168) | | | |
|---|---|---|---|
| When? | Where? | Description and contact info | Admission |
| Mid Jul., Fri. 7-11pm, Sat. 7-11pm, Sun. 11am-5pm | 6021 W. Lincoln Ave., West Allis | Festival of live music, special dinner each day, and more. http://www.stritawestallis.org/Festival | Free |

| MUSKEGO COMMUNITY FESTIVAL--MUSKEGO (Su 169) | | | |
|---|---|---|---|
| When? | Where? | Description and contact info | Admission |
| Late Aug., Thu. 6-10pm, Fri. 5-11:30pm, Sat. 12-11:30pm, Sun. 11am-6pm | Veterans Memorial Park, W182-S8200 Racine Ave., Muskego | Largest free admission festival in SE Wisconsin, featuring live entertainment, parade, food, drinks, midway, and more. http://www.muskegofest.com/ | Free |

| FALLS FEST—MENOMONEE FALLS (Su 170) | | | |
|---|---|---|---|
| When? | Where? | Description and contact info | Admission |
| Late Jul., Thu., Fri., Sat., Sun. (see website for hours) | Village Park, Garfield Drive, Menomonee Falls | Festival of live entertainment, food, beverages, and more. https://www.facebook.com/Menomonee-Falls-Fest-136324016389307/ | Free |

| ST. JOHN THE EVANGELIST FAMILY FESTIVAL--GREENFIELD (Su 171) | | | |
|---|---|---|---|
| When? | Where? | Description and contact info | Admission |
| Late Jul., Fri. 5-11pm, Sat. 3-11pm, Sun. 12-9pm | 8500 W. Cold Spring Road, Greenfield | Festival including rides, games, wine cellar, bingo, food, music, and more. http://www.stjohns-grfd.org/ | Free |

## ST ROBERT FAIR--SHOREWOOD (Su 172)

| When? | Where? | Description and contact info | Admission |
|---|---|---|---|
| Early Jun., Sat. 12-10pm, Sun. 12-7pm | 2200 E. Capitol Drive, Shorewood | Fair including world famous minnow races, food, bouncy house, children's games, rummage, raffle, live music, and more. http://www.shorewoodwi.com/news-events/st-robert-fair | Free |

## THIENSVILLE-MEQUON LIONSFEST (Su 173)

| When? | Where? | Description and contact info | Admission |
|---|---|---|---|
| Mid Jun., Fri., Sat., Sun. (see website for hours) | Thiensville Village Park, 250 Elm St., Thiensville | Festival of food, carnival rides, softball, bingo, live entertainment. http://www.e-clubhouse.org/sites/thiensville/ | Free, $5 for entertainment tent |

## ST. THOMAS COUNTRY FAIR--WATERFORD (Su 174)

| When? | Where? | Description and contact info | Admission |
|---|---|---|---|
| Early Jun., Thu. 4:30-11pm, Fri. 4-11pm, Sat. 4:30-11:30pm, Sun. 11am-4pm | St. Thomas Aquinas, 305 S. First St., Waterford | Family fair including raffle, face/balloon sculpting, rides, food, silent auctions, and more. http://www.stthomascountryfair.com/sunday.html | Free |

## MONUMENT SQUARE ART FESTIVAL--RACINE (Su 175)

| When? | Where? | Description and contact info | Admission |
|---|---|---|---|
| Mid Jun., Sat. 10am-5pm, Sun. 10am-4pm | Downtown Racine | Festival of exhibiting artists, art contests, art for sale, http://www.monumentsquareartfest.com/ | Free |

## ST. ALOYSIUS FESTIVAL—WEST ALLIS (Su 176)

| When? | Where? | Description and contact info | Admission |
|---|---|---|---|
| Early Jun., Fri. 5-11pm, Sat. 12-11pm, Sun. 11:30am-8pm | 1414 S. 93rd St., West Allis | Festival of food, bands, rides, face painting, raffle, clowns and Pokerino. http://www.westalliscatholicparishes-west.org/ | Free |

## ST. JOHN NEUMANN FESTIVAL--WAUKESHA (Su 177)

| When? | Where? | Description and contact info | Admission |
|---|---|---|---|
| Early Jun., Fri. 4:30pm-12am, Sat. 12pm-12am, Sun. 12-4pm | 2400 W. Hwy 59, Waukesha | Festival of food, live music, carnival rides, bake sale, fireworks, and more. https://www.facebook.com/sjnfestival | Free |

| QUEEN OF APOSTLES FESTIVAL--PEWAUKEE (Su 178) | | | |
|---|---|---|---|
| **When?** | **Where?** | **Description and contact info** | **Admission** |
| Early Jun., Fri. 4-11pm, Sat. 9am-11pm, Sun. 11:30am-6pm | N35-W23360 Capitol Drive, Pewaukee | Festival of live music, food, carnival rides, raffle, and more. http://www.queenofapostles.net/Parish-Festival | Free |

| CEDARBURG PLEIN AIR PAINTING COMPETITION SHOW & SALE (Su 179) | | | |
|---|---|---|---|
| **When?** | **Where?** | **Description and contact info** | **Admission** |
| Mid Jun., Thu. 10am-5pm, Fri. 10am-5pm, Sat. 10am-7pm | Cedarburg Cultural Center, W62-N546 Washington Ave., Cedarburg | Opportunity to see or purchase works of 150 artists painting scenic Ozaukee County, special pricing times, and party. http://pleinaircedarburg.blogspot.com/ | Free |

| DELAFIELD BLOCK PARTY (Su 180) | | | |
|---|---|---|---|
| **When?** | **Where?** | **Description and contact info** | **Admission** |
| Early Jul., Fri. 5pm-12am, Sat. 5pm-12am | Downtown Delafield | Party including large beverage tent, portable bars, food, live music. http://www.visitdelafield.org/event-calendar/block-party/ | Free |

| CEDARBURG WOMAN'S CLUB GARDEN WALK (Su 181) | | | |
|---|---|---|---|
| **When?** | **Where?** | **Description and contact info** | **Admission** |
| Early Jul., Sat., Sun. (see website for hours) | Varying locations in Cedarburg; see website | Walk through beautiful gardens with chance to purchase plants and garden art pieces, raffle. http://www.cedarburgwomansclub.org/garden-walk-2016.html | $10 |

| SWEET APPLE-WOOD FESTIVAL--CUDAHY (Su 182) | | | |
|---|---|---|---|
| **When?** | **Where?** | **Description and contact info** | **Admission** |
| Late Jul, Fri. 3-11:30pm, Sat. 12-11:30pm, Sun. 11am-8pm | Cudahy Park, 3000 E. Ramsey Ave., Cudahy | Festival of carnival rides, raffles, live music, food, beverage, and more. https://www.facebook.com/events/1097407450316732/ | Free |

| PEWAUKEE LAKE WATER SKI CLUB SHOW--PEWAUKEE (Su 183) | | | |
|---|---|---|---|
| **When?** | **Where?** | **Description and contact info** | **Admission** |
| Jun. to early Sep., Thu.'s 6:45pm; some Sat.'s & Mon.'s 5:30pm | Lakefront Park, Pewaukee | Show of skilled water skiing on beautiful lake. http://plwsc.org/ | Free |

| FIESTA WAUKESHA (Su 184) | | | |
|---|---|---|---|
| **When?** | **Where?** | **Description and contact info** | **Admission** |
| Mid Jun., Fri. 4-11pm, Sat./Sun. 11am-11pm | Frame Park, 1240 Frame Park Drive, Waukesha | Ethnic festival held on the banks of the Fox River of cuisine, music, children's area, rides, and more. http://www.travelwisconsin.com/events/history-heritage/fiesta-waukesha-40109 | Free |

## DOMINIC DAYS--BROOKFIELD (Su 185)

| When? | Where? | Description and contact info | Admission |
|---|---|---|---|
| Mid Jul., Thu. 5-10pm, Fri. 5-11pm, Sat. 1-11pm, Sun. 12-6pm | St. Dominic Catholic Church, 18255 W. Capitol Drive, Brookfield | Festival with car show, rides, steeplechase/run/walk, food, live music, and much more. http://www.stdominic-brookfield.org/Community/DominicDays.asp | Free |

## GRILLIN' IN GRAFTON (Su 186)

| When? | Where? | Description and contact info | Admission |
|---|---|---|---|
| Early Jul., Fri., Sat. (see website for hours) | Centennial Park, 1370 17th Ave., Grafton | Event featuring a KCBS BBQ competition, live music, dance, parade, fireworks, music, and more family fun. http://grilliningrafton.com/ | Free |

## MIDSUMMER FESTIVAL OF THE ARTS--SHEBOYGAN (Su 187)

| When? | Where? | Description and contact info | Admission |
|---|---|---|---|
| Mid Jul., Sat., 10am-5pm; Sun. 12-5pm | 608 New York Ave., Sheboygan | Festival with food and over 130 artists exhibiting paintings, wood carvings, photos, jewelry, furniture, ceramics, glass and more. http://visitsheboygan.com/event/midsummer-festival-of-the-arts/ | Free |

## HOLY ANGELS FESTIVAL OF ANGELS—WEST BEND (Su 188)

| When? | Where? | Description and contact info | Admission |
|---|---|---|---|
| Mid Jun., Fri. 5-11:30pm, Sat. 12-11:30pm, Sun. 11am-9pm | 138 N. 8th Ave., West Bend | Festival with music, mini golf, games, midway, raffle, and more. http://hawb.org/festival-of-angels/ | Free |

## BOHEMIAN FEST--RACINE (Su 189)

| When? | Where? | Description and contact info | Admission |
|---|---|---|---|
| Mid Jun., Fri. 6:30-10:30pm, Sat. 7-11pm, Sun. 12-3:30pm | St. John Nepomuk Parish, 1903 Green St., Racine | Music, food, games, kids' fest, bake sale, traditional Bohemian pork roast with sauerkraut and dumpling dinner will be served at 4 p.m. Saturday until sold out. http://racinecountyeye.com/calendar/ | $10 (for Bohemian dinner) |

## GERMAN NIGHT--PLYMOUTH (Su 190)

| When? | Where? | Description and contact info | Admission |
|---|---|---|---|
| Late Jul., Thu. evening | Plymouth City Park, Plymouth | Evening of foot-stomping German music, bands, roast pig, other foods and beverages. http://plymouthwisconsin.com/family.html | Free |

## TASTE OF LAKE COUNTRY--PEWAUKEE (Su 191)

| When? | Where? | Description and contact info | Admission |
|---|---|---|---|
| Late Jul., Fri. 5-10:30pm, Sat. 3-10:30pm | Lakefront Park, 222 W. Wisconsin Ave., Pewaukee | Festival of food, music, art, shopping, and more near Pewaukee Lake. http://tasteoflakecountry.com/ | Free |

## OLD FALLS VILLAGE DAYS—MENOMONEE FALLS (Su 192)

| When? | Where? | Description and contact info | Admission |
|---|---|---|---|
| Early Jun., Sat. 8am-4pm, Sun. 10am-4pm | Old Falls Village Museum, N96-W15791 County Line Road, Menomonee Falls | Event with vehicles from the past, tour of Old Falls Village Museum, children's area, auctions, music, and more. http://www.oldfallsvillage.com/events-2/old-falls-village-days/ | Free |

## LAKE COUNTRY ART FESTIVAL--DELAFIELD (Su 193)

| When? | Where? | Description and contact info | Admission |
|---|---|---|---|
| Early Jul., Sat. 9am-4pm | Naga-Waukee Park, Highway 83, Delafield | Art festival with scores of artists exhibiting jewelry, pottery, furniture, paintings, wearables, and more. http://www.lakecountrywomensclub.org/art-festival.html | $5 per carload |

## CROATIAN DAY--MUKWONAGO (Su 194)

| When? | Where? | Description and contact info | Admission |
|---|---|---|---|
| Early Jul. Sat. 11am-8pm | Mukwonago Field Park, Highway 83 and NN, Mukwonago | Festival of Croatian food, art, bakery, music, and more (not just for Croatians). http://cfulodge993.org/festival/ | Free |

## ST. RITA FAMILY FESTIVAL--RACINE (Su 195)

| When? | Where? | Description and contact info | Admission |
|---|---|---|---|
| Mid Aug., Fri., Sat., Sun. (see website for hours) | 4339 Douglas Ave., Racine | Festival with big name entertainment, games, food, wrist band rides, and more. http://wisconsinfestivals.org/node/1476 | Free |

## DELAFIELD FOOD AND MUSIC FESTIVAL (Su 196)

| When? | Where? | Description and contact info | Admission |
|---|---|---|---|
| Early Jul., Fri. & Sat. 5pm-12am | Main St., Delafield | Two back-to-back evenings that feature a large beverage tent with portable bars scattered around the festival grounds, specialty beer, wine, and assorted beverages with food and live music. http://chamber.visitdelafield.org/events | Free |

## WAUKESHA COUNTY FAIR--WAUKESHA (Su 197)

| When? | Where? | Description and contact info | Admission |
|---|---|---|---|
| Late Jul., Wed. thru Sun. (most days 10am-midnight) | Waukesha Expo Grounds, 1000 Northview Rd., Waukesha | A celebration of Waukesha's rural heritage with barnyard animals, crafts, foods, farm displays—and, of course, a midway. http://www.waukeshacountyfair.com/ | $10, $5 kids 6-12, free kids <6 |

## LITTLE WONDERS--FRANKLIN (Su 198))

| When? | Where? | Description and contact info | Admission |
|---|---|---|---|
| Jun.-Aug., select Mon.'s 9:30-10:30am 3-year olds; 11-12 3-year olds | Wehr Nature Center, 9701 W College Ave, Franklin | Story, paint with mud (disguised as finger paint), snack, puddle-jumping walk, making mud pies. Register at http://www.friendsofwehr.org/childrens-programs/early-childhood/ | $10 per child (with adult); $7 if Milw. Co. resident |

| GIRO D'GRAFTON (Su 199) | | | |
|---|---|---|---|
| When? | Where? | Description and contact info | Admission |
| Mid Jun., Sat. 11:30am-8:30pm | Downtown Grafton | Screaming spectator bike race of .85 miles, part of the Tour of America's Dairyland race series. http://www.celebrategrafton.com/Giro.html | Free (as spectator) |

| BROWN DEER EAT & GREET ON THE STREET (Su 200) | | | |
|---|---|---|---|
| When? | Where? | Description and contact info | Admission |
| Early Jun., Sat. 3-11pm | Deerwood Dr. and Brown Deer Rd. Brown Deer | Festival with artist and community marketplace, children's games, live entertainment, food, obstacle course. http://www.browndeerwi.org/events-5/eat-greet-street/ | Free |

| MENOMONEE FALLS FARMERS MARKET (Su 201) | | | |
|---|---|---|---|
| When? | Where? | Description and contact info | Admission |
| Jun. thru Aug. Wed. 8am-3pm, Sun. 9am-2pm | North Junior HS parking lot, Main St. (one block west of Appleton Ave.) | Fresh produce from Wisconsin farmers, baked goods, arts, crafts. http://menomoneefallsdowntown.com/ | Free |

| WEST ALLIS ALA CARTE (Su 202) | | | |
|---|---|---|---|
| When? | Where? | Description and contact info | Admission |
| Early Jun., first Sun. (see webpage for hours) | Greenfield Ave. between 70th-76th St., West Allis | Event to showcase the downtown West Allis business district and offer activities including face painting, music, food vendors, and more. http://www.westalliswi.gov/index.aspx?NID=411 | Free |

| DIVINE MERCY FUNFEST—SOUTH MILWAUKEE (Su 203) | | | |
|---|---|---|---|
| When? | Where? | Description and contact info | Admission |
| Early Jul., Fri. 4:30-11:30pm, Sat. 2-11:30pm, Sun. 12-5pm | 695 College Ave., South Milwaukee | Food and variety of bands (food runs $10-$12). http://www.dmfunfest.com/ | Free |

| SOUTH MILWAUKEE LIONSFEST (Su 204) | | | |
|---|---|---|---|
| When? | Where? | Description and contact info | Admission |
| Late Jul., Fri., Sat., Sun. (see website for hours) | 16th and Rawson Aves., South Milwaukee | Festival including car cruise, fish dinner, rib dinner, live music, family day, and more. http://www.smlions.org/lionsfest/ | Free |

| ST. JOSEPH FUN FEST—BIG BEND (Su 205) | | | |
|---|---|---|---|
| When? | Where? | Description and contact info | Admission |
| Mid Aug., Fri., Sat , Sun. (see website for hours) | S89-W22650 Milwaukee Ave., Big Bend | Festival including food, raffles, rummage sale, music, games. http://www.stjoesbb.com/parish/outreach/activities/ | Free |

| HOLY APOSTLES FAMILY FESTIVAL—NEW BERLIN (Su 206) | | | |
|---|---|---|---|
| When? | Where? | Description and contact info | Admission |
| Late Jun., Fri. 5-10:30pm, Sat. 3-10:30pm, Sun.12:15-6:30pm | 16000 W. National Ave., New Berlin | Festival of music, food, rides, bingo, and more. http://www.hanb.org/ | Free |

| RUMBLE BY THE RIVER—BIG BEND (Su 207) | | | |
|---|---|---|---|
| When? | Where? | Description and contact info | Admission |
| Early Jul., Fri. 4-10pm, Sat. 4-11pm | Big Bend Village Park, Big Bend | Truck and tractor pull, Friday night fish fry, kids' dash for cash, classic car show (additional cost). https://www.facebook.com/BigBendPull | $10 adults, free kids ≤ 12 |

| OLD FALLS VILLAGE CIVIL WAR ENCAMPMENT—MENOMONEE FALLS (Su 208) | | | |
|---|---|---|---|
| When? | Where? | Description and contact info | Admission |
| Mid Jul., Sat., Sun. 8am-5pm | Old Falls Village Museum, N96-W15791 County Line Road, Menomonee Falls | Weekend of Civil War activities including Union Drill/Artillery, Civil War music, flag raising, train depot robbery, children's scavenger hunt, field hospital demonstrations, and more. http://www.oldfallsvillage.com/events-2/civil-war-encampment/ | $8, $2 kids 5-12, free <5 |

| GREENDALE VILLAGE DAYS (Su 209) | | | |
|---|---|---|---|
| When? | Where? | Description and contact info | Admission |
| Mid Aug., Fri. 5-9pm, Sat. 2:30-9pm, Sun. 1-4pm | Downtown Greendale | Festival of live bands, beer tent, food, bingo, magic show, games, midway carnival rides, and more. http://greendaleentertainment.com/village-days/ | Free |

| WAUKESHA OLD CAR CLUB SHOW & PICNIC (Su 210) | | | |
|---|---|---|---|
| When? | Where? | Description and contact info | Admission |
| Mid Aug., Sun. 8am-3:30pm | Frame Park, Waukesha | WOCC Car show with beverages, food, live music. http://www.waukeshaoldcarclub.org/calendars_events.html | Free to spectators |

| WILSON CENTER GUITAR COMPETITION & FESTIVAL--BROOKFIELD (Su 211) | | | |
|---|---|---|---|
| When? | Where? | Description and contact info | Admission |
| Mid Aug., Thu. 3-9pm, Fri. 9am-9pm, Sat. 9am-9pm | 19805 W. Capitol Drive, Brookfield | Multi-genre festival that features four different competitions—Rock/Blues, Fingerstyle, Jazz, and classical. http://www.wilson-center.com/guitar-fest-competitor-information/ | Free for most performances |

| WASHINGTON COUNTY FAIR—WEST BEND (Su 212) | | | |
|---|---|---|---|
| When? | Where? | Description and contact info | Admission |
| Late Jul., Tue. thru Sun. (hours vary) | Washington County Fair and Conference Center, 3000 Hwy. PV., West Bend | Music, music, music, tractor pull, fireworks, and special activities for vets and seniors. http://www.wcfairpark.com/fair/ | $3 on Tue. 7 & up ($7-$10 other days); free kids <7 |

## WISCONSIN STATE FAIR--$2 THURSDAY—WEST ALLIS (Su 213)

| When? | Where? | Description and contact info | Admission |
|---|---|---|---|
| Early Aug., Thu. (promotion ends at 4pm) | Wisconsin State Fair, 640 S. 84th St., West Allis | Barnyard animals, crafts, live music, big name entertainers, food, exhibits, and, of course, a midway. http://wistatefair.com/fair/ | $2 with 2 non-perishable food items or donation |

## WISCONSIN STATE FAIR—FAMILY FUN MONDAY—WEST ALLIS (Su 214)

| When? | Where? | Description and contact info | Admission |
|---|---|---|---|
| Early Aug., Mon. 8am-6pm | Wisconsin State Fair, 640 S. 84th St., West Allis | Barnyard animals, crafts, live music, big name entertainers, food, exhibits, and, of course, a midway. http://wistatefair.com/fair/ | $5 adults, free kids <12 |

## OCONOMOWOC FESTIVAL OF THE ARTS (Su 215)

| When? | Where? | Description and contact info | Admission |
|---|---|---|---|
| Late Aug., Sat. 10am-5pm, Sun. 10am-5pm | Fowler Park, Oconomowoc | Festival including visual art, performances, a youth stage, live music, and more. http://www.oconomowocarts.org/ | Free |

## CEDARBURG STRAWBERRY FESTIVAL (Su 216)

| When? | Where? | Description and contact info | Admission |
|---|---|---|---|
| Late Jun., Sat. 10am-6pm, Sun. 10am-5pm | Downtown Cedarburg | An art-filled weekend centered on strawberries, including every variety of fruit delicacies, other foods, and art exhibits. http://www.cedarburgfestival.org/ | Free |

## SCOTTISH HIGHLAND GAMES--WAUWATOSA (Su 217)

| When? | Where? | Description and contact info | Admission |
|---|---|---|---|
| Early Jun., Sat. 9am-10pm | Hart Park, State St. & 70th St., Wauwatosa | Event with live music, a parade of Tartans, highland dancing, piping, sheepdog demonstrations, haggis taco-eating contests, horse exhibitions, and axe throwing competitions. http://milwaukeescottishfest.com/ | $10, free kids <13, military in uniform. |

## RUMMAGE-A-RAMA—WEST BEND (Su 218)

| When? | Where? | Description and contact info | Admission |
|---|---|---|---|
| Mid Jun., Sat. 1-4pm, Sun. 1-3pm | Washington County Fair Park & Conference Center, 3000 Highway PV, West Bend | Antiques, crafts, rummage from dealers, businesses, and the community. http://rummage-a-rama.com | $5 adults, free kids <12 |

## NATIONAL NIGHT OUT--GREENFIELD (Su 219)

| When? | Where? | Description and contact info | Admission |
|---|---|---|---|
| First week Aug., weekday 5:30-8:30pm | Konkel Park, 5151 W. Layton Ave., Greenfield | Fun evening of free food, games, rides, chance to dialogue with local police and community organizations, http://www.safesound.org/contact-us/ (or local TV websites) | Free |

## NATIONAL NIGHT OUT—HALES CORNERS (Su 220)

| When? | Where? | Description and contact info | Admission |
|---|---|---|---|
| Early Aug., weekday 5-9pm | Hales Corners Park: 5765 S. New Berlin Rd., Hales Corners | Fun evening of free food, games, rides, chance to dialogue with local police and community organizations, http://www.safesound.org/events/national-night-out-events-across-milwaukee/ | Free |

## BUTLER FARMERS MARKET (Su 221)

| When? | Where? | Description and contact info | Admission |
|---|---|---|---|
| Early Jun.-late Aug., Mon. 12-6pm | Hampton Ave. at 127th St. | Fresh produce from Wisconsin farmers, baked goods, arts, crafts, activities. https://www.facebook.com/Butler-City-Farmers-Market-161364660572913/ | Free |

## THURSDAY NIGHT THUNDER—WEST ALLIS (Su 222)

| When? | Where? | Description and contact info | Admission |
|---|---|---|---|
| Late Aug., 2:30-sunset | Milwaukee Mile, 640 S. 84th St., West Allis | High performance driving sessions on the Milwaukee Mile Road Course (non-competitive). http://wistatefair.com/wsfp/events/ | Free |

## ARTISTS IN THE GARDEN—HALES CORNERS (Su 223)

| When? | Where? | Description and contact info | Admission |
|---|---|---|---|
| Late Aug., Sat., Sun. 10am-5pm | Boerner Botanical Gardens, 9400 Boerner Dr., Hales Corners | Art fair and plein air competition, horticultural exhibitions, food, live music. http://county.milwaukee.gov/ParksCalendar | Free |

## - -NATIONAL NIGHT OUT--FRANKLIN (Su 224)

| When? | Where? | Description and contact info | Admission |
|---|---|---|---|
| Early Aug., weekday 6-9pm | Franklin Public Library, 9151 W. Loomis Rd., Franklin | Fun evening of free food, games, rides, chance to dialogue with local police and community organizations, http://www.safesound.org/events/national-night-out-events-across-milwaukee/ | Free |

## ANNUAL GARDEN WALK—HALES CORNERS (Su 225)

| When? | Where? | Description and contact info | Admission |
|---|---|---|---|
| Early Jun., Wed. 6:30-8pm | Boerner Botanical Gardens, 9400 Boerner Dr, Hales Corners; meet at the gift shop | Expert-led walks with rotating topics, 90 minutes long. http://boernerbotanicalgardens.org/event/ | $5 suggested donation |

## ST. MARY PARISH FESTIVAL—HALES CORNERS (Su 226)

| When? | Where? | Description and contact info | Admission |
|---|---|---|---|
| Early Jul., Fri., Sat., Sun., see website for hours | 9520 W. Forest Home Ave., Hales Corners | Festival to bring parishioners together in a spirit of community, including food, games, concessions, live music, raffle and more. http://www.stmaryhc.org/page.php?id=234 | Free |

## ST. AGNES PARISH FESTIVAL--BUTLER (Su 227)

| When? | Where? | Description and contact info | Admission |
|---|---|---|---|
| Late Aug., Fri. 4-11pm, Sat. 11am-11pm | 12801 W. Fairmount Ave, Butler | Festival of craft beers, food, live music, auction, games, talent show, and more. http://www.stagnesparish.org/parish/events.cfm | Free |

## ST. MATTHIAS FESTIVAL—WEST ALLIS (Su 228)

| When? | Where? | Description and contact info | Admission |
|---|---|---|---|
| Late Aug., Fri. 5-11pm, Sat. 12-11pm, Sun. 2-8pm | 9306 W. Beloit Rd., West Allis | Festival of food, live music, adult & kids games, Sheepshead tournament, rides, and more. http://www.stmatthias-milw.org/committees/festival/ | Free |

## ST. JAMES FAMILY FEST--MUKWONAGO (Su 229)

| When? | Where? | Description and contact info | Admission |
|---|---|---|---|
| Late Aug., see website for times | 830 County Road NN East, Mukwonago | Festival of music, food, games, children's activities, and more. http://www.stjamesmukwonago.org/ | Free |

## WATERFORD BALLOON FESTIVAL (Su 230)

| When? | Where? | Description and contact info | Admission |
|---|---|---|---|
| Mid Jul., Fri. 4-8pm, Sat. 6am-9pm, Sun. 6am-10am | Main St., Waterford | Festival of hot air balloons, dancers, helicopter rides, food, live entertainment. http://www.waterford-wi.org/waterford_balloon_fest.html | Free |

## ST. LOUIS PARISH FESTIVAL-CALEDONIA (Su 231)

| When? | Where? | Description and contact info | Admission |
|---|---|---|---|
| Late Aug., Sat. 6-11pm, Sun. 11am-6pm | 13207 County Road G, Caledonia | Festival of food, classic cars, games, rides, and more. http://www.stlouisparishwi.com/festival/index.html | Free |

## IOLA CAR SHOW & SWAP MEET (Su 232)

| When? | Where? | Description and contact info | Admission |
|---|---|---|---|
| Early Jul., Thu., Fri., Sat., check website for times | Highway 161, Iola | One of the biggest car shows/swap meets in America, featuring 2500 show cars, 4200 swap spaces, http://iolaoldcarshow.com/ | Free |

## SLOVAK-AMERICAN DAY--FRANKLIN (Su 233)

| When? | Where? | Description and contact info | Admission |
|---|---|---|---|
| Late Jul., Sun., see website for time | Croatian Park, 9140 S. 76th St., Franklin | Festival of Slovak/Czech food, handicrafts, art, and children's activities. https://foursquare.com/v/slovakamerican-day-festival/4e2c6d5bd4c0e5c89acf0ed1 | Free |

| DONNA LEXA MEMORIAL ART FAIR--WALES (Su 234) | | | |
|---|---|---|---|
| **When?** | **Where?** | **Description and contact info** | **Admission** |
| Late Aug., Sat. 9am-4pm | Along the Glacial Drumlin bike trail, Wales | Fair committed to excellence in fine arts, plus food, children's activities, live music, and more. http://www.donnalexamemorialartfair.org/ | Free |

| XAVIERAN MISSION FESTIVAL--FRANKLIN (Su 235) | | | |
|---|---|---|---|
| **When?** | **Where?** | **Description and contact info** | **Admission** |
| Late Jun., Sat., 3-11pm, Sun. 12-7pm | 4500 Xavier Drive, Franklin | Festival of food, clowns, face painting, game booths, raffle, live music, bouncing castle. https://www.facebook.com/xmfestival/ | Free |

| MILL STREET FEVSTIAL--PLYMOUTH (Su 236) | | | |
|---|---|---|---|
| **When?** | **Where?** | **Description and contact info** | **Admission** |
| Early Jul., Sat. 9-4pm | Mill Street, downtown Plymouth | Festival including live music, pony rides, petting zoo, dunk tank, and more. https://www.facebook.com/events/929174723865284/ | Free |

| NATIONAL NIGHT OUT--MUSKEGO (Su 237) | | | |
|---|---|---|---|
| **When?** | **Where?** | **Description and contact info** | **Admission** |
| First week Aug., weekday 5-9pm | Veterans Park, W128S8200 Racine Ave., Muskego | Fun evening of free food, games, rides, chance to dialogue with local police and community organizations, http://www.safesound.org/events/national-night-out-events-across-milwaukee/ | Free |

| NATIONAL NIGHT OUT--BROOKFIELD (Su 238) | | | |
|---|---|---|---|
| **When?** | **Where?** | **Description and contact info** | **Admission** |
| First week Aug., weekday 5-9pm | Brookfield Civic Plaza, 2000 N. Calhoun Rd., Brookfield | Fun evening of free food, games, rides, chance to dialogue with meet local police and community organizations, http://www.safesound.org/events/national-night-out-events-across-milwaukee/ | Free |

| NATIONAL NIGHT OUT—SOUTH MILWAUKEE (Su 239) | | | |
|---|---|---|---|
| **When?** | **Where?** | **Description and contact info** | **Admission** |
| Mid Aug., weekday 5:30-9pm | South Milwaukee Police Dept., 2424 15th Ave., South Milwaukee | Fun evening of free food, games, rides, chance to dialogue with local police and community organizations, http://www.safesound.org/events/national-night-out-events-across-milwaukee/ | Free |

| NATIONAL NIGHT OUT--CUDAHY (Su 240) | | | |
|---|---|---|---|
| **When?** | **Where?** | **Description and contact info** | **Admission** |
| First week Aug., weekday, 4-8pm | Cudahy Family Library, 9151 W. Loomis Rd., Cudahy | Fun evening of free food, games, chance to dialogue with local police and community organizations, http://www.safesound.org/events/national-night-out-events-across-milwaukee/ | Free |

| NATIONAL NIGHT OUT--OCONOMOWOC (Su 241) | | | |
|---|---|---|---|
| **When?** | **Where?** | **Description and contact info** | **Admission** |
| First week Aug., weekday, 5-8pm | Pabst Farms YMCA, 1750 E. Valley Rd., Oconomowoc | Fun evening of free food, games, rides, chance to dialogue with local police and community organizations, http://www.safesound.org/events/national-night-out-events-across-milwaukee/ | Free |

| NATIONAL NIGHT OUT--MUKWONAGO (Su 242) | | | |
|---|---|---|---|
| **When?** | **Where?** | **Description and contact info** | **Admission** |
| First week Aug., weekday 6-8:30 pm | Field Park at Park View Middle School, 930 N. Rochester St., Mukwonago | Fun evening of free food, games, rides, chance to dialogue with local police and community organizations, http://www.safesound.org/events/national-night-out-events-across-milwaukee/ | Free |

| NATIONAL NIGHT OUT--GLENDALE (Su 243) | | | |
|---|---|---|---|
| **When?** | **Where?** | **Description and contact info** | **Admission** |
| First week Aug., weekday 5:30-8pm | Glendale Fire Station, 5901 N. Milwaukee River Pkwy., Glendale | Fun evening of free food, games, chance to dialogue with local police and community organizations, http://www.safesound.org/events/national-night-out-events-across-milwaukee/ | Free |

| NATIONAL NIGHT OUT--WAUWATOSA (Su 244) | | | |
|---|---|---|---|
| **When?** | **Where?** | **Description and contact info** | **Admission** |
| First week Aug., weekday 6-8pm | Celebrations throughout city, Wauwatosa | Fun evening of free food, games, rides, chance to dialogue with local police and community organizations, http://www.safesound.org/events/national-night-out-events-across-milwaukee/ | Free |

| NATIONAL NIGHT OUT—ZOO WAUWATOSA (Su 245) | | | |
|---|---|---|---|
| **When?** | **Where?** | **Description and contact info** | **Admission** |
| First week Aug., weekday 4-8pm | Milwaukee County Zoo, 10001 W Bluemound Rd., Wauwatosa | Fun evening of free food, games, rides, animals, chance to dialogue with local police and community organizations, http://www.safesound.org/events/national-night-out-events-across-milwaukee/ | Free, pre-registration required |

# Fall: September, October, November (not in chronological order)

> Listings do NOT include classes, workouts, or clubs
>
> LISTINGS ONLY INCLUDE RECURRING EVENTS UNDER $10 PER ADULT ADMISSION. THE ADMISSION PRICE ONLY COVERS THE ENTRANCE FEES AND DOES NOT INCLUDE THE PRICE OF FOOD, RIDES, GOODS, RAFFLE TICKETS, OR OTHER ITEMS THAT MAY BE PART OF THE EVENT.
>
> PLEASE ALWAYS CHECK THE CONTACT INFO FOR ANY RECENT CHANGES IN THESE EVENTS.

## National Holiday-Specific

## Labor Day

| LABOR DAY PARADE (Fa 1) | | | |
|---|---|---|---|
| **When?** | **Where?** | **Description and contact info** | **Admission** |
| Labor Day, 11am-12pm | Zeidler Square (downtown) to Summerfest grounds | Parade of labor riders in their trucks, on their bikes, and marching, with floats with labor themes. http://milwaukeelabor.org/events/laborfest/ (see parade route on website) | Free |

| ANNUAL LABOR DAY DOGGIE DIP (Fa 2) | | | |
|---|---|---|---|
| **When?** | **Where?** | **Description and contact info** | **Admission** |
| Labor Day, 4:30-6 pm | Greenfield Park, 2028 S. 124th St. | Opportunity to let dogs play in pool before it is drained. https://milwaukeedogparks.org/doggie-dip/ | $5 per dog |

| LABORFEST (Fa 3) | | | |
|---|---|---|---|
| **When?** | **Where?** | **Description and contact info** | **Admission** |
| Labor Day, begins at noon | Maier Festival Park, 639 E. Summerfest Pl. | Festival to celebrate the labor force in Milwaukee, including vendors, exhibits, food. http://milwaukeelabor.org/events/laborfest/ | Free |

| ST. BONIFACE FALL FESTIVAL--GERMANTOWN (Fa 4) | | | |
|---|---|---|---|
| **When?** | **Where?** | **Description and contact info** | **Admission** |
| Early Sep., Fri. 4-8pm, Sat. 8am-11pm, Sun. 8am-10:30pm | W204-N11940 Goldendale Road, Germantown | Labor Day weekend festival of music, food, car show, raffle, and fellowship. http://www.stbonifacewi.org/Fall-Festival | Free |

| OAK CREEK LIONSFEST (Fa 5) | | | |
|---|---|---|---|
| When? | Where? | Description and contact info | Admission |
| Early Sep., Fri. starts 3pm, Sat. 12pm, Sun. 9am, Mon. 12pm | 9327 S. Shepard Ave., Oak Creek | Labor Day long weekend festival with food, Brew City Wrestling, raffle, midway rides, and more. http://www.oakcreeklionsfestival.com/ | Free |

| ST. FRANCIS DAYS (Fa 6) | | | |
|---|---|---|---|
| When? | Where? | Description and contact info | Admission |
| Labor Day weekend, Thu. 6-10pm, Fri. 6-11pm, Sat., Sun. 12-11pm | 4230 S. Kirkwood, St. Francis | Days of family activities, music, health walk, chicken dinner, animal exhibits, food all day and night. http://stfrancisdays.com/ | Free |

# Halloween/Day of the Dead

| TRICK-OR-TREAT STREET (Fa 7) | | | |
|---|---|---|---|
| When? | Where? | Description and contact info | Admission |
| Late Oct., Sat. 12-2pm | National Ave. between 31st & 39th | A scary afternoon or-trick-or-treating that includes a costume contest, bouncy houses, and more (kids must be accompanies by adult). Contact Gisela at 414-385-5336 or gisela@lbwn.org | Free |

| CARVING FOR PUMPKIN PAVILION (Fa 8) | | | |
|---|---|---|---|
| When? | Where? | Description and contact info | Admission |
| Mid. Oct., Tue., Wed. Thu. 5-9pm | Humboldt Park, 3000 S Howell Ave. | Pumpkin carvings, displays, music, food, and more. http://county.milwaukee.gov/ParksCalendar | Free |

| GHOSTS UNDER GLASS (Fa 9) | | | |
|---|---|---|---|
| When? | Where? | Description and contact info | Admission |
| Late Oct., Fri. 6-9pm | Mitchell Park Domes, 524 S Layton Blvd. | A not-too-spooky night of family fun with treats and ghostly fun. http://county.milwaukee.gov/ParksCalendar | $8, $5 kids 3-17, free kids $\leq$ 2 |

| DIA DE LOS MUERTOS (Fa 10) | | | |
|---|---|---|---|
| When? | Where? | Description and contact info | Admission |
| Late Oct., Sat. 10am-4pm | Walker's Square Park, 9th & Mineral | Day of celebration, parade, games, other events. http://county.milwaukee.gov/ParksCalendar | Free |

| HALLOWEEN IN COOPER PARK (Fa 11) | | | |
|---|---|---|---|
| When? | Where? | Description and contact info | Admission |
| Late Oct., Sat. 11am-1pm | Cooper Park, 86th & Locust | Halloween celebration. http://county.milwaukee.gov/ParksCalendar | Free |

| HAUNTED HALLS (Fa 12) | | | |
|---|---|---|---|
| When? | Where? | Description and contact info | Admission |
| Late Oct., Thu. 6-8pm, Fri. 6-8pm | Neighborhood House, 2819 W. Richardson Pl. | Scary Halloween tour of haunted halls, first come/first serve. www.neighborhoodhousemke.org | $3 or donation of 2 non-perishable food |

| HALLOWEEN GLEN (Fa 13) | | | |
|---|---|---|---|
| When? | Where? | Description and contact info | Admission |
| Mid Oct., Fri.5:45-7:30pm | Pick-up location at MPS Central at 5225 W. Vliet St. (rear parking lot) | Educational and interactive skits to celebrate Halloween. Register to attend at http://milwaukeerecreation.net/rec/Special-Events/Halloween-Glen.htm | $6 |

| LATINO FAMILY EXPO & FESTIVAL (Fa 14) | | | |
|---|---|---|---|
| When? | Where? | Description and contact info | Admission |
| Late Oct., Sat. 12-6pm | St. Anthony's High School, 4807 S. 2nd St. | A Health, Education, and Employment Fair to honor Latinos/as, featuring social services, entertainment, immigration counseling, trick or treats, consumer products, and more. https://www.facebook.com/events/675815075900340/ | Free |

| NIGHT OUT TRICK OR TREAT (Fa 15) | | | |
|---|---|---|---|
| When? | Where? | Description and contact info | Admission |
| Late Oct., Sat. 6-8pm | Manitoba Park, 49th & Manitoba | Halloween celebration. http://county.milwaukee.gov/ParksCalendar | Free |

| HALLOWEEN AT GREENFIELD PARK—WEST ALLIS (Fa 16) | | | |
|---|---|---|---|
| When? | Where? | Description and contact info | Admission |
| Late Oct., Sat. 4-8pm | Greenfield Park, S. 116th & Greenfield, West Allis | Halloween celebration. http://county.milwaukee.gov/ParksCalendar | Free |

| HALLOWEEN HAUNTS--FRANKLIN (Fa 17) | | | |
|---|---|---|---|
| When? | Where? | Description and contact info | Admission |
| Mid. Oct., Sat; hikes start every 7 minutes, 6:30-8:30pm | Wehr Nature Center, 9701 W College Ave, Franklin, | Halloween Haunts that educate families about misunderstood nature in a kooky, slightly spooky way. http://county.milwaukee.gov/ParksCalendar | $10 |

| ZOMBIE HOUSE AT THE MILL POND—SOUTH MILWAUKEE (Fa 18) | | | |
|---|---|---|---|
| When? | Where? | Description and contact info | Admission |
| Late Oct., Fri., Sat. 5:30-8:30pm | East Oak Creek Parkway and Mill Rd., South Milwaukee | Spooky Halloween event. http://county.milwaukee.gov/ParksCalendar | Free |

## Veterans' Day

| VETERANS DAY PARADE (Fa 19) | | | |
|---|---|---|---|
| **When?** | **Where?** | **Description and contact info** | **Admission** |
| Early Nov., Sat. 11am | Parade begins at Kilbourn Ave. & Plankinton Ave. | Parade honoring veterans, beginning at Plankinton & Kilbourn, runs on E. Wells to the War Memorial Center and finally to Veterans Park. http://www.honorourmilitary.us/veterans-day-parade/ | Free |

## Thanksgiving

| THANKSGIVING DINNER (Fa 20) | | | |
|---|---|---|---|
| **When?** | **Where?** | **Description and contact info** | **Admission** |
| Late Nov., Tue, 5:30-7:30pm | Neighborhood House, 2819 W. Richardson Pl. | Turkey provided if you bring trimmings to share. Register with Tasha at (414) 933-6161 x142 www.neighborhoodhousemke.org | Free with donated canned goods |

| NOT A CREATURE WAS STIRRING—HOLIDAY FLORAL SHOW (Fa 21) | | | |
|---|---|---|---|
| **When?** | **Where?** | **Description and contact info** | **Admission** |
| Mid-late Nov., Mon.-Fri. 9am-5pm; Sat., Sun. holidays 9am-4pm | Mitchell Park Domes, 524 S. Layton Blvd. | Holiday floral show at the Horticultural Center. http://county.milwaukee.gov/ParksCalendar | $7, $5 students, disabled, 6-18; free 6 |

## General

| DOORS OPEN MILWAUKEE (Fa 22) | | | |
|---|---|---|---|
| **When?** | **Where?** | **Description and contact info** | **Admission** |
| Late Sep., Sat. thru Sun. | Sites all over greater Milwaukee | Event opens the doors to over 100 buildings that hold hidden treasures and special stories, from churches to office buildings, theaters to work sites, museums to hotels, clubs to universities; all sites of historic, architectural, cultural, or commercial interest. http://doorsopenmilwaukee.org/ | Free |

| SAINTS PETER & PAUL BLOCK PARTY (Fa 23) | | | |
|---|---|---|---|
| **When?** | **Where?** | **Description and contact info** | **Admission** |
| Mid Sep., Sat. 12-9pm | SS Peter & Paul Parish, 2491 N. Murray Ave. | Day of music, games, raffles, auction, food. http://ssppmilw.org/blockparty/ | Free |

| WALKING TOUR—HISTORIC MILWAUKEE DOWNTOWN (Fa 24) | | | |
|---|---|---|---|
| **When?** | **Where?** | **Description and contact info** | **Admission** |
| Sep.-mid Oct., 10am | Meets in street level lobby of the Plankinton Building at 161 W. Wisconsin Ave. | Tour that explores the architecture and streetscape to gain insight into how the commercial use of the rivers, lake, and harbor helped create the Milwaukee of today. http://historicmilwaukee.org/walking-tours/ | $10 adults, $2 kids 7-17, free kids 6 and under |

| WALKING TOUR—RIVER WALK (Fa 25/26) | | | |
|---|---|---|---|
| When? | Where? | Description and contact info | Admission |
| Sep.-mid Oct., Thu.'s 5:30pm | Tour meets in the park at the northwest corner of East St. Paul Ave. and North Water St. | Opportunity to learn about the design concepts used to create the Riverwalk's unique path and enjoy the outdoor sculptures dotting the Riverwalk landscape. http://historicmilwaukee.org/walking-tours/ | $10 adults, $2 kids 7-17, free kids 6 and under |

| WALKING TOUR—HISTORIC THIRD WARD (Fa 27) | | | |
|---|---|---|---|
| When? | Where? | Description and contact info | Admission |
| Sep.-mid Oct., Sat.'s, 11am | Meets by the Bublr bike station in front of the Commission House at 400 N. Broadway | Opportunity to learn about the wonderfully designed warehouses and the diverse group of industries that thrived in them in the Third Ward. http://historicmilwaukee.org/walking-tours/ | $10 adults, $2 kids 7-17, free kids 6 and under |

| HUNTING MOON POW WOW (Fa 28) | | | |
|---|---|---|---|
| When? | Where? | Description and contact info | Admission |
| Mid Oct., Fri. opens at 3pm, Sat. opens at 10am, Sun. opens at 10am | UW-M Panther Arena, 400 W. Kilbourn Ave. | American Indian pow wow, dance competition, art, crafts, grand entry. http://www.huntingmoonpowwow.com/ | Under $10 |

| RIVERWEST ART WALK (Fa 29) | | | |
|---|---|---|---|
| When? | Where? | Description and contact info | Admission |
| Early Oct., Sat. all day | Get tickets and maps at Art Bar (722 E. Burleigh St.), Jazz Gallery (926 E. Center St.), and Riverwest Food Co-op (733 E. Clarke St.) | A walk that features artist studios, beautiful gardens, and various sanctuaries. ericoortiz55@gmail.com or http://www.riverwestart.org/artwalk-2015.html | $5, $3 kids and seniors |

| OKTOBERFEST AT TOSA FARMERS MARKET (Fa 30) | | | |
|---|---|---|---|
| When? | Where? | Description and contact info | Admission |
| Late Sep., check website for times | Café Bavaria, 7700 Harwood Ave. | German food, music, festivities. http://www.cafebavaria.com/ | Free |

| MILWAUKEE COUNTY WINTER FARMERS MARKET (Fa 31) | | | |
|---|---|---|---|
| When? | Where? | Description and contact info | Admission |
| Nov., Sat. 9am-12:30pm | Mitchell Park Domes, 524 S. Layton Blvd. | Fresh produce, meat, eggs, dairy from Wisconsin small farms. http://www.mcwfm.org/ | Free |

| THIRD WARD ART FESTIVAL (Fa 32) | | | |
|---|---|---|---|
| When? | Where? | Description and contact info | Admission |
| Early Sep., Sat., Sun. 10am-6pm | On Broadway between St. Paul & Menomonee Sts. | Showcase of more than 140 juried artists, with live music, food, and activities for children. http://amdurproductions.com/third-ward-art-festival/ | Free |

## WALKING TOUR—BRADY STREET (Fa 33)

| When? | Where? | Description and contact info | Admission |
|---|---|---|---|
| Sep.-mid Oct. Sat.'s 1:30pm | Meets in front of Three Holy Women Catholic Parish (St. Hedwig Church) at 1702 N. Humboldt Ave. | Tour through the neighborhood on a half-mile stroll and learn about the area's Polish and Italian roots, the counter culture of the '60s and '70s and the area's recent urban renaissance. http://historicmilwaukee.org/walking-tours/ | $10 adults, $2 kids 7-17, free kids 6 and under |

## WALKING TOUR—BAY VIEW (Fa 34)

| When? | Where? | Description and contact info | Admission |
|---|---|---|---|
| Sep.-mid Oct, Sun.'s 1pm | Meets by the Bublr bike station at Zillman Park, 2180 S Kinnickinnic Ave. | Opportunity to learn the story of how Bay View began with a patchwork of industry and diverse group of immigrants and grew to the charming neighborhood you see today. http://historicmilwaukee.org/walking-tours/ | $10 adults, $2 kids 7-17, free kids 6 and under |

## ANNUAL STARVING ARTISTS SALE (Fa 35)

| When? | Where? | Description and contact info | Admission |
|---|---|---|---|
| Mid Sep., Sun. 10am-5pm | Mount Mary University campus, 2900 Menomonee River Parkway | Sale of works in all media of local and national artists for $100 or less. http://www.mtmary.edu/alumnae/events/starving-artists-show.html | $10, presale |

## RIVERWEST GARDENERS MARKET (Fa 36)

| When? | Where? | Description and contact info | Admission |
|---|---|---|---|
| Sep.-mid Oct., Sun. 10am-3pm | Garden Park, 821 E. Locust St., | Fresh produce from Wisconsin farmers, baked goods, arts, crafts. https://riverwestmarket.wordpress.com/ | Free |

## GALLERY NIGHT AND DAY (Fa 37)

| When? | Where? | Description and contact info | Admission |
|---|---|---|---|
| Late Oct., Fri. 5-9pm, Sat. 10am-4pm | Check web page. | Milwaukee's two-day premier art event for both the experienced art connoisseur and most beginning admirers that features 50 venues to explore throughout the downtown Milwaukee area four times a year. http://www.historicthirdward.org/events/gallerynight.php | Free |

## WESTOWN FARMERS MARKET (Fa 38)

| When? | Where? | Description and contact info | Admission |
|---|---|---|---|
| Sep.-late Oct., Wed. 10am-2pm | Zeidler Union Square, 301 W. Michigan St. | Fresh produce from Wisconsin farmers, baked goods, art, music, crafts. http://westown.org/neighborhood-events/westown-farmers-market/ | Free |

| ST. GREGORY THE GREAT FESTIVAL (Fa 39) | | | |
|---|---|---|---|
| When? | Where? | Description and contact info | Admission |
| Early Sep., Thu., Fri., Sat , Sun. (see website for hours) | 3160 S. 63rd St. | Four days including games for all ages, live music, food, raffle. https://www.everfest.com/e/st-gregory-the-great-parish-festival-milwaukee-wi | Free |

| MILWAUKEE COFFEE FESTIVAL PRESENTED BY PENDULUM COFFEE (Fa 40) | | | |
|---|---|---|---|
| When? | Where? | Description and contact info | Admission |
| Early Nov., Sat. 10am-3pm | Urban Ecology Center, 1500 E. Park Pl. | A day of tasting, experiencing and learning about sustainably grown and locally sold coffee from the leaders in the field. Register early. http://urbanecologycenter.org/programs-events-main.html | Free |

| SOUTH SHORE FARMERS MARKET (Fa 41) | | | |
|---|---|---|---|
| When? | Where? | Description and contact info | Admission |
| Sep..-late Oct., Sat. 8am-12pm | South Shore Park, 2900 South Shore Dr. | Fresh produce from Wisconsin farmers, baked goods, art, crafts, music, demonstrations. https://www.facebook.com/South-Shore-Farmers-Market-352715301468098/ | Free |

| CATHEDRAL SQUARE MARKET (Fa 42) | | | |
|---|---|---|---|
| When? | Where? | Description and contact info | Admission |
| Sep.-early Oct., Sat. 9am-1pm | 520 E. Wells St. | Fresh produce from Wisconsin farms, baked goods, crafts, art, live music, yoga and activities. http://easttown.com/events/cathedral-square-market | Free |

| HARAMBE COMMUNITY MARKET (Fa 43) | | | |
|---|---|---|---|
| When? | Where? | Description and contact info | Admission |
| Sep.-early Oct., Sat. 12-4pm | Rose Park, 3045 N. MLK Jr. Dr. | Fresh food from Wisconsin farms, baked goods, crafts, art. http://www.hgnimke.org/harambee-community-market | Free |

| JACKSON PARK FARMERS MARKET (Fa 44) | | | |
|---|---|---|---|
| When? | Where? | Description and contact info | Admission |
| Early Sep., Thu. 3:30-7pm | 3300 W. Forest Home Ave. | Fresh food from Wisconsin farms, baked goods, crafts, art. http://jacksonpark.us/farmers-market/ | Free |

| WALKER'S SQUARE FARMERS MARKET (Fa 45) | | | |
|---|---|---|---|
| When? | Where? | Description and contact info | Admission |
| Sep.-early Oct., Sun., Thu. 8am-5pm | 1031 S. 9th St. | Fresh produce from Wisconsin farmers, baked goods, art, crafts. http:// walkersquare.org/farmers-market/ | Free |

| FONDY'S FARMERS MARKET—SCHLITZ PARK (Fa 46) | | | |
|---|---|---|---|
| When? | Where? | Description and contact info | Admission |
| Sep.-early Oct. (see website for hours) | Schlitz Park | Fresh produce from Wisconsin farmers, baked goods, art, music, crafts. http://fondymarket.org | Free |

| GRACE FINE ART & CRAFT FESTIVAL (Fa 47) | | | |
|---|---|---|---|
| When? | Where? | Description and contact info | Admission |
| Early Nov., Sun. 9am-3pm | Grace Evangelical Lutheran Church, 1209 N. Broadway | Over 25 fine artists with original work for great Christmas shopping opportunity. http://www.gracedowntown.org/whatsnew/ | Free |

| SATURDAY PRESCHOOL SERIES (Fa 48) | | | |
|---|---|---|---|
| When? | Where? | Description and contact info | Admission |
| Autumn, Sat.'s 10:30-11:30am | Riverside Park 1500 E. Park Pl. | For youngsters, ages 3-5 years old with adult to enjoy exploring nature together, including a mix of seasonal indoor and outdoor play, songs, and stories--dress for playing outdoors. http://urbanecologycenter.org/programs-events-main.html | $7, free kids 3-5 |

| MILWAUKEE RUNNING FESTIVAL (Fa 49) | | | |
|---|---|---|---|
| When? | Where? | Description and contact info | Admission |
| Early Nov., Sun. 6:45am-3pm | Veterans Park, on Lake Michigan | Running events for all ages and all abilities to participate in or to watch (mile, half mile, 5K, marathon, half marathon). http://www.milwaukeerunningfestival.com/ | Free (to watch only) |

| ANNUAL HEALTH FEST (Fa 50) | | | |
|---|---|---|---|
| When? | Where? | Description and contact info | Admission |
| Mid Oct., Sat. 11am-2pm | Neighborhood House, 2819 W. Richardson Pl. | Health and breast cancer screenings, yoga, Zumba, roller skating, art therapy, and more. www.neighborhoodhousemke.org | Free |

| ROLLER SKATING NIGHTS (Fa 51) | | | |
|---|---|---|---|
| When? | Where? | Description and contact info | Admission |
| Sep. thru Nov., every 3rd Fri. 6-8pm | Our Savior's Lutheran Church, 3022 W. Wisconsin Ave. | Roller skating and skate rentals. www.neighborhoodhousemke.org | Free with 2 non-perishable food items |

| FALL FAMILY PADDLE (Fa 52) | | | |
|---|---|---|---|
| When? | Where? | Description and contact info | Admission |
| Mid Sep., Sat., 1-3pm | Washington Park 1859 N. 40th St. | Celebration of autumn with guided canoeing and nature on lovely lagoon. Requires early registration. http://urbanecologycenter.org/programs-events-main.html | $9 adult, $6 kids (with adult) |

| OKTOBERFEST AT PERE MARQUETTE (Fa 53) | | | |
|---|---|---|---|
| When? | Where? | Description and contact info | Admission |
| Late Sep. to early Oct., Fri., Sat. opens noon, Sun. opens 10am | Pere Marquette Park and Marcus Center grounds | Opportunity to enjoy German food, beer, and music along Riverwalk. http://www.marcuscenter.org/calendar/month/ | Free |

| FAMILY HIKE (Fa 54/55) | | | |
|---|---|---|---|
| When? | Where? | Description and contact info | Admission |
| Nov., Tue.'s, 4-6pm | Menomonee Valley, 3700 W. Pierce St. | Guided hike to see changes in seasons through Three Bridges Park. http://urbanecologycenter.org/programs-events-main.html | Free, but might need to register |

| ENCHANTED FOREST (Fa 56) | | | |
|---|---|---|---|
| When? | Where? | Description and contact info | Admission |
| Late Oct., Sat. 5:30-7:30pm | Riverside Park 1500 E. Park Pl. | Opportunity to see Riverside Park come alive with nocturnal characters. http://urbanecologycenter.org/programs-events-main.html | $9, $7 kids |

| MILWAUKEE SHORT FILM FESTIVAL (Fa 57) | | | |
|---|---|---|---|
| When? | Where? | Description and contact info | Admission |
| Early Sep., Fri., Sat., see website for hours | Comedy Sports 420 S. 1st St. | Wide variety of independent short films. http://www.milwaukeeindependentfilmsociety.org/ | $10 |

| BAY VIEW BASH (Fa 58) | | | |
|---|---|---|---|
| When? | Where? | Description and contact info | Admission |
| Mid Sep., Sat. 11am-10pm | Between Potter and Clement on Kinnickinnic Ave. | A Community Festival of food, art, music, crafts, books, and community organizations. http://www.bayviewbash.org/ | Free |

| MILWAUKEE LGBT FILM FESTIVAL (Fa 59) | | | |
|---|---|---|---|
| When? | Where? | Description and contact info | Admission |
| Mid Oct., see website for times | Union Cinema, 2200 E. Kenwood Blvd. | Wide variety of films and documentaries with LGBT themes. http://uwm.edu/lgbtfilmfestival/events/ | $10 (Union Cinema screenings only) |

| SILVER CITY INTERNATIONAL FOOD AND ART WALK (Fa 60) | | | |
|---|---|---|---|
| When? | Where? | Description and contact info | Admission |
| Late Sep., Sat., 12-5pm | W. National Ave. between 33rd St.& 35th St. | Festival to celebrate the diversity of the Silver City neighborhood. http://www.lbwn.org/ | Free |

| GARDEN DISTRICT FARMERS MARKET (Fa 61) | | | |
|---|---|---|---|
| When? | Where? | Description and contact info | Admission |
| Early Sep.- mid Oct., Sat.'s 1-5pm | Just south of Howard on 6th St. | Market of fresh vegetables and other vendors. http://www.milwaukeegdna.com/ | Free |

| GUEST LECTURE SERIES ON THE ARTS (Fa 62) | | | |
|---|---|---|---|
| **When?** | **Where?** | **Description and contact info** | **Admission** |
| Autumn, most Wed.'s 7:30-9pm | Art Center Lecture Hall, 2400 E. Kenwood Blvd. | Lectures on a variety of art-related topics including visual art, film, mythology, performance, story-telling, photography, and more. http://psoacal.uwm.edu/events/ | Free |

| FONDY FARMERS MARKET (Fa 63) | | | |
|---|---|---|---|
| **When?** | **Where?** | **Description and contact info** | **Admission** |
| Early Sep.-early Nov. Sat./Sun. 8am-3pm | 2200 W. Fond du Lac Ave. | Fresh produce from Wisconsin farmers, baked goods, arts, crafts, activities. http://fondymarket.org/ | Free |

| INDIAN SUMMER (Fa 64) | | | |
|---|---|---|---|
| **When?** | **Where?** | **Description and contact info** | **Admission** |
| Early Sep., Fri. 4pm-12am, Sat., 12pm-12am, Sun. 11am-8pm | 639 E. Summerfest Pl. | Celebration of Native American traditions, music, food, music, pow wow, kids' activities. http://www.indiansummer.org/advanced-tickets/ | $10 if purchased before July 30 |

| RENT A BIKE AT VETERANS PARK (Fa 65) | | | |
|---|---|---|---|
| **When?** | **Where?** | **Description and contact info** | **Admission** |
| Sep. to mid Oct., Sat.'s, Sun.'s, late am to sunset | Veterans Park, 1400 N. Lincoln Memorial Dr. | Bicycle riding along Milwaukee's lakefront. http://www.wheelfunrentals.com/Locations/Milwaukee-2 | $10 adults bikes (cruiser or mountain); $5 kids' bikes |

| UMOS MEXICAN INDEPENDENCE DAY PARADE (Fa 66) | | | |
|---|---|---|---|
| **When?** | **Where?** | **Description and contact info** | **Admission** |
| Mid Sep., Sun. 10am-12pm | Starts at 20th & Oklahoma Ave. (see route on website) | Southside parade of arts, floats, local organizations honoring Mexican Independence Day. http://www.umos.org/special_events/mexican_independence.html | Free |

| UMOS MEXICAN INDEPENCE DAY FESTIVAL (Fa 67) | | | |
|---|---|---|---|
| **When?** | **Where?** | **Description and contact info** | **Admission** |
| Mid Sep., Sun. 12-8pm | UMOS Center, 2701 S. Chase Ave. | Festival of food vendors, beer, live music, craft vendors, everything Mexican. http://www.umos.org/special_events/mexican_independence.html | Free |

| PADDLE BOAT RENTALS (Fa 68) | | | |
|---|---|---|---|
| **When?** | **Where?** | **Description and contact info** | **Admission** |
| Sep. thru Oct., daily 10am-7pm, weather permitting | Juneau Park, 801 N. Lincoln Memorial Dr. | Paddle boating with views of Milwaukee skyline and Lake Michigan. http://juneauparkpaddleboats.com/fleet.html | $5 per person per half hour, if < 16 need parental consent |

| SAIL BOAT RENTALS (Fa 69) | | | |
|---|---|---|---|
| When? | Where? | Description and contact info | Admission |
| Sep. thru Oct., daily 10am-7pm, weather permitting | Juneau Park, 801 N. Lincoln Memorial Dr. | Sail boating with views of Milwaukee skyline and Lake Michigan. http://juneauparkpaddleboats.com/fleet.html | $5 per boat per half hour, if < 16 need parental consent |

| HOLIDAY PAJAMA JAMBOREE (Fa 70) | | | |
|---|---|---|---|
| When? | Where? | Description and contact info | Admission |
| Late Nov., Wed., 7pm | Bradley Pavilion of the Marcus Center, 929 N. Water St. | One-hour classical pops concert geared toward children and their families, with pajamas, teddy bears, and blankets are welcome for the youngest audience members. http://festivalcitysymphony.org/concerts/pajama-jamborees/ | Free, but nonperishable food donations encouraged |

| BRADY STREET PET PARADE (Fa 71) | | | |
|---|---|---|---|
| When? | Where? | Description and contact info | Admission |
| Oct., check website for times | Brady Street | Brady Street Pet Parade, with vendors, http://bradystreet.org/documents/41-pet-parade | Free |

| MARQUETTE WOMEN'S BASKETBALL (Fa 72/73) | | | |
|---|---|---|---|
| When? | Where? | Description and contact info | Admission |
| Nov. (regular season) | Al McGuire Center, 770 N. 12th St. | Marquette University women's basketball games. http://www.gomarquette.com/sports/w-baskbl/sched/marq-w-baskbl-sched.html | $5 and $10 |

| MILWAUKEE BUCKS GAMES (Fa 74) | | | |
|---|---|---|---|
| | Where? | Description and contact info | Admission |
| Late Oct. thru Nov. (regular season) | BMO Harris Bradley Center, 1001 N. 4th St. | Games of Milwaukee Bucks of the National Basketball Association. http://www.nba.com/bucks/ | Some tickets at $9 and $10 |

| POETRY IN THE PARK (Fa 75) | | | |
|---|---|---|---|
| When? | Where? | Description and contact info | Admission |
| Sep., select Tue.'s, 6:30-8pm (check website) | Juneau Park, Prospect Ave. & Kilbourn Ave., near Juneau statue | Poetry readings by known poets. https://www.facebook.com/Juneau-Park-Friends-113584992257/ | Free |

| MARQUETTE GOLDEN EAGLES GAMES (Fa 76) | | | |
|---|---|---|---|
| When? | Where? | Description and contact info | Admission |
| Nov. (regular season) | BMO Harris Bradley Center, 1001 N. 4th St. | Marquette University men's basketball games. http://www.gomarquette.com/tickets/m-baskbl-main.html | Some tickets at $5 and $10 |

| FAMILY FREE DAY AT THE ZOO (Fa 77) | | | |
|---|---|---|---|
| When? | Where? | Description and contact info | Admission |
| Early Oct., Nov., select Sat.'s, 9:30am-4:30pm | Milwaukee County Zoo, 10001 W. Bluemound Rd. | If you want to stay warm, we have many indoor animal exhibits for your enjoyment. If you're more of the outdoorsy type, you'll also find many outdoor animal exhibits. http://www.milwaukeezoo.org/events/ | Free |

| HARVEST FEST AT THE LIBRARY (Fa 78) | | | |
|---|---|---|---|
| When? | Where? | Description and contact info | Admission |
| Early Oct., Sat., 10am-1pm | MPL Central Library, 814 W. Wisconsin Ave. | Opportunity to celebrate the turning of the season with live entertainment, pumpkins, cookie decorating, face painting, storytelling, live animals, and crafts. http://www.mpl.org/services/events/ | Free |

| CENTER STREET PARK FALL FEST (Fa 79) | | | |
|---|---|---|---|
| When? | Where? | Description and contact info | Admission |
| Mid Oct. Sat., 11am-4pm | Center St. Park, 6420 W. Clarke St. | Chance to enjoy music, food, face painting, pumpkin bowling, sack racing, mural making, and much more. http://www.centerstreetpark.com/fall-fest/ | Free |

| FROMM PET FEST (Fa 80) | | | |
|---|---|---|---|
| When? | Where? | Description and contact info | Admission |
| Late Sep., Sat. 10am-6pm | Henry Maier Festival Grounds, 639 E. Summerfest Pl. | Opportunity to provide cats and dogs with entertainment, training, samples. http://petfestmke.com/ | Free |

| TOUR OF JONES ISLAND WATER RECLAMATION FACILITY (Fa 81) | | | |
|---|---|---|---|
| When? | Where? | Description and contact info | Admission |
| During Doors Open Milwaukee, late Sep., Sat., 10am-5pm | Meet: Jones Island Water Reclamation Facility, corner of E. Jones St. & Harbor Dr., Jones Island | Choice of 1 hour or 30 minute tour of Water Reclamation Facility to learn how the facility produces a fertilizer as the by-product of the water reclamation process—Milorganite. http://www.mmsd.com | Free |

| GRANVILLE BID CAR, TRUCK, AND BIKE SPECTACULAR (Fa 82/83) | | | |
|---|---|---|---|
| When? | Where? | Description and contact info | Admission |
| Late Sep., Sun. 10am-3pm | Russ Darrow, 7676 N. 76th St. | Exhibition of iconic custom vehicles, food trucks. http://www.granvillebusiness.org/granville-bid.html | Free |

| FALL FLORAL SHOW (Fa 84) | | | |
|---|---|---|---|
| When? | Where? | Description and contact info | Admission |
| Late Sep. to early Nov., Mon.-Fri. 9am-5pm, Sat. 9am-4pm | Mitchell Park Domes, 524 S Layton Blvd. | Fall harvest festival and floral exhibits. http://county.milwaukee.gov/ParksCalendar | $5-$7, $3-$5 kids 6-17, seniors, disabled, free kids <6 |

| OKTOBERFEST ARTISAN FAIR (Fa 85) | | | |
|---|---|---|---|
| When? | Where? | Description and contact info | Admission |
| Mid Oct., Fri. 4-8pm, Sat. 11am-8pm, Sun. 12-4pm | Our Lady of Lourdes, 3722 S. 58th St. | A celebration of creativity, community, and harvest including music, fish fry, champagne brunch, artisan shopping. http://www.ololmke.org/oktoberfest/ | Free |

| STORY TIME AT THE DOMES (Fa 86) | | | |
|---|---|---|---|
| When? | Where? | Description and contact info | Admission |
| Mid. Oct. to early Nov., Mon.'s 10:30-11am | Mitchell Park Domes, 524 S Layton Blvd. | Children's stories about autumn, perfect for the home-schooled. http://county.milwaukee.gov/ParksCalendar | Free kids 3-8 accompanied by adult |

| SKYWAUKEE WALKING TOUR (Fa 87) | | | |
|---|---|---|---|
| When? | Where? | Description and contact info | Admission |
| Oct. 24-Dec. 12, usually Sat. 1pm | Meets in street level lobby of the Plankinton Building, 161 W. Wisconsin Ave. | Historic Milwaukee Inc. tour that explores the architectural and cultural history of Milwaukee's landmarks while staying indoors;. http://historicmilwaukee.org/walking-tours/ | $10 adults; $2 kids 7-17, free kids under 7 |

■■■■■■■■■■■■■■■■■■■■■■■■■■■■■■■■■■■■■■■■■■■■■■■■■■■

| HOLIDAY FOLK FAIR INTERNATIONAL--WEST ALLIS (Fa 88) | | | |
|---|---|---|---|
| When? | Where? | Description and contact info | Admission |
| Mid November, Fri.-Sun. (see schedule on website) | State Fair Park Expo Center; 8200 W. Greenfield Ave., West Allis | Multicultural festival of music, food, dance, and the arts. www.folkfair.org/index.html | $10 adults in advance, seniors, kids 6-12, free kids <6 |

## ANNUAL SCANDINAVIAN FESTIVAL—NEW BERLIN (Fa 89)

| When? | Where? | Description and contact info | Admission |
|---|---|---|---|
| Early Oct., Sat. 10am-6pm | Ronald Reagan High School, 4225 S. Calhoun Rd., New Berlin | Festival of arts/crafts, genealogy services, live music, dancing, fashion show, food, and Children's Parade. http://www.norwayhouse-milw.org/events.html | $7 adults, $2 kids 4-12, free kids <4 |

## MENOMONEE FALLS FARMERS MARKET (Fa 90)

| When? | Where? | Description and contact info | Admission |
|---|---|---|---|
| Sep., Oct., Wed. 8am-3pm, Sun. 9am-2pm | North Junior HS parking lot, Main St. (one block west of Appleton Ave.) | Fresh produce from Wisconsin farmers, baked goods, arts, crafts. http://menomoneefallsdowntown.com/ | Free |

## HORSE EXPO—WEST ALLIS (Fa 91)

| When? | Where? | Description and contact info | Admission |
|---|---|---|---|
| Mid Sep., Thu. 7am-9pm, Fri. 7am-5pm, Sat. 7am-9pm, Sun. 7am-1pm | Wisconsin State Fair Park, 640 S. 84th, West Allis | Wisconsin State 4-H horse expo including English and Western pleasure, showmanship, trail, and more. http://wistatefair.com/wsfp/events/ | Free |

## WEST ALLIS FARMERS MARKET (Fa 92)

| When? | Where? | Description and contact info | Admission |
|---|---|---|---|
| Sep.-late Nov., Tue. 12-6pm, Sat. 1-6pm | 6501 W. National Ave. | Fresh produce from Wisconsin farmers; baked goods, arts, crafts. https://www.facebook.com/westallisfarmersmarket/ | Free |

## BROOKFIELD FARMERS MARKET (Fa 93)

| When? | Where? | Description and contact info | Admission |
|---|---|---|---|
| Sep.-late Oct., Sat. 7:30am-12pm | 2000 N. Calhoun Rd. | Fresh produce from Wisconsin farmers; arts/crafts fair every third Sun. of month. http://www.brookfieldfarmersmarket.com/ | Free |

## MAKER FAIRE MILWAUKEE—WEST ALLIS (Fa 94)

| When? | Where? | Description and contact info | Admission |
|---|---|---|---|
| Late Sep., Sat. 9am-6pm, Sun. 10am-5pm | Wisconsin State Fair Park, 640 S. 84th, West Allis | Showcase of invention, creativity, tech enthusiasts, crafters, artists, educators, tinkerers, students and others. www.makerfairemilwaukee.com | Free |

| ANNUAL BONSAI EXHIBIT—HALES CORNERS (Fa 95) | | | |
|---|---|---|---|
| **When?** | **Where?** | **Description and contact info** | **Admission** |
| Mid Sep., Fri. 6-10pm, Sat. 11am-5pm, Sun. 10am-3pm | Boerner Botanical Gardens, 9400 Boerner Dr, Hales Corners | Opportunity to experience the art of the bonsai tree and the ancient art of miniature trees. http://county.milwaukee.gov/ParksCalendar | Free |

| RUMMAGE-A-RAMA—WEST BEND (Fa 96) | | | |
|---|---|---|---|
| **When?** | **Where?** | **Description and contact info** | **Admission** |
| Mid Oct., Sat. 1-4pm, Sun. 1-3pm | Washington County Fair Park & Conference Center, 3000 Highway PV, West Bend | Antiques, crafts, rummage from dealers, businesses, and the community. http://rummage-a-rama.com | $5 adults, free kids <12 |

| LITTLE WONDERS--FRANKLIN (Fa 97) | | | |
|---|---|---|---|
| **When?** | **Where?** | **Description and contact info** | **Admission** |
| Sep., Oct., select Mon.'s 9:30-10:30am 3-year olds; 11-12 3-year olds | Wehr Nature Center, 9701 W College Ave, Franklin | Story, paint with mud (disguised as finger paint), snack, puddle-jumping walk, making mud pies. Register at http://www.friendsofwehr.org/childrens-programs/early-childhood/ | $10 per child (with adult); $7 if Milw. Co. resident |

| TOSAFEST--WAUWATOSA (Fa 98) | | | |
|---|---|---|---|
| **When?** | **Where?** | **Description and contact info** | **Admission** |
| Mid Sep., Fri. 6-11:30pm, Sat. 11:30am-11:30pm | 7615 W. State St. Wauwatosa | Opportunity to enjoy festival that extends Wauwatosa's 40-year tradition of music, food, and family fun, to celebrate our historic village and community spirit.   www.tosafest.org/ | Free |

| WELLNESS, BODY, MIND & SPIRIT EXPO—BROWN DEER (Fa 99) | | | |
|---|---|---|---|
| **When?** | **Where?** | **Description and contact info** | **Admission** |
| Late Oct. Sun. 10am-5pm | Four Points by Sheraton, 8900 North Kildeer Ct., Brown Deer | The latest in new thought presentations, advances in alternative health, and the nation's finest psychics and *mediums.* http://www.wellnessbodymindspirit.com/ | $5 |

| TOSA FARMERS MARKET (Fa 100) | | | |
|---|---|---|---|
| **When?** | **Where?** | **Description and contact info** | **Admission** |
| Sep.-mid Oct., Sat. 8am-12pm | 7720 Harwood Ave., Wauwatosa | Fresh produce from Wisconsin farmers, baked goods, arts, crafts. http://tosafarmersmarket.com/ | Free |

| OKTOBERFEST--GLENDALE (Fa 101) | | | |
|---|---|---|---|
| **When?** | **Where?** | **Description and contact info** | **Admission** |
| Early Sep. to early Oct., Fri.'s, Sat's, see website for hours | Heidelberg Park, 700 W Lexington Blvd., Glendale | Fest of traditional German brass bands, Schuhplatter folk dancing, singing, yodeling, sing-alongs, broiled chicken, bratwurst, spanferkel, rollbraten, pretzels, and more. http://www.funtober.com/oktoberfest/wisconsin/ | $5; free for kids |

| OKTOBERFEST--CEDARBURG (Fa 102) | | | |
|---|---|---|---|
| **When?** | **Where?** | **Description and contact info** | **Admission** |
| Early Oct., Sat. and Sun., see website for hour | Community Center Parking Lot, W63 N641 Washington Ave. | Fest with specialty beers from Hofbrau, Hacker Pschorr, Leinenkugel, Bluemoon, authentic German dinners including wiener schnitzel, bratwurst, currywurst, and other dishes, live entertainment. http://www.funtober.com/oktoberfest/wisconsin/ | Free |

| OKTOBERFEST AT WHITNALL PARK BEER GARDEN--GREENDALE (Fa 103) | | | |
|---|---|---|---|
| **When?** | **Where?** | **Description and contact info** | **Admission** |
| Early Oct., Sat.'s 11am-6pm | Root River Parkway Picnic Area 1A, Greendale | Festival of live German and other music, beer, food. http://county.milwaukee.gov/ParksCalendar | Free |

| CEDARBURG WINE & HARVEST FESTIVAL (Fa 104) | | | |
|---|---|---|---|
| **When?** | **Where?** | **Description and contact info** | **Admission** |
| Late Sep., Sat.10am-6pm, Sun. 10am-5pm | Cedar Creek Settlement, N70-W6340 Bridge Road, Cedarburg | Festival of wine, harvest crops, classic cars, farmers market, live music, contests, and more. http://www.cedarburg.org/event/1465450-wine-harvest-festival-2016 | Free |

| SCOTTISH HIGHLAND GAMES—WISCONSIN--WAUKESHA (Fa 105) | | | |
|---|---|---|---|
| **When?** | **Where?** | **Description and contact info** | **Admission** |
| Early Sep., Fri. 5-10pm; Sat. daytime | Waukesha Expo Center, 1000 Northview Rd. | Event with live music, a parade of Tartans, highland dancing, piping, sheepdog demonstrations, haggis taco-eating contests, horse exhibitions, and axe throwing competitions. http://www.wisconsinscottish.org/info | $10, free kids <13 |

| BUTLER FARMERS MARKET (Fa 106) | | | |
|---|---|---|---|
| **When?** | **Where?** | **Description and contact info** | **Admission** |
| Early Sep.-mid Oct., Mon. 12-6pm | Hampton Ave. at 127th St. | Fresh produce from Wisconsin farmers, baked goods, arts, crafts, activities. https://www.facebook.com/Butler-City-Farmers-Market-161364660572913/ | Free |

| HARVEST FAIR—WEST ALLIS (Fa 107) | | | |
|---|---|---|---|
| **When?** | **Where?** | **Description and contact info** | **Admission** |
| Late Sep., Fri. 5-11pm, Sat. 9am-11pm, Sun. 9am-5pm | State Fair Park, 640 S. 84th St., West Allis | Autumn fair that features rides, food, games such as pumpkin bowling, and contests such as the pumpkin chuckin'. http://wistatefair.com/harvestfair/ | Free |

| HARVEST OF ARTS AND CRAFTS--GREENDALE (Fa 108) | | | |
|---|---|---|---|
| When? | Where? | Description and contact info | Admission |
| Mid Sep., Sat., Sun. 10am-4pm | Trimborn Farm 8881 W. Grange Ave., Greendale | A festival that features some of the most exceptional hand-crafted work in the Midwest. http://www.milwaukeehistory.net/historic-sites-2/trimborn-farm/harvest-festival-of-arts-crafts/ | $5, free for kids 10 & under |

| CRAFT & RELIC--FRANKLIN (Fa 109) | | | |
|---|---|---|---|
| When? | Where? | Description and contact info | Admission |
| Mid Nov., Sat., Sun. 10am-4pm | Milwaukee County Sports Complex, 6000 Ryan Rd., Franklin | Event with over 150 vendors from across the Midwest, filling their booths with vintage, salvages, industrial, handmade, hand-forged, modern, antiqued, up-cycled, and repurposed goods, including furniture, clothing, garden items, pottery, and more. http://www.recraftandrelic.com/attend.html | $8 and up; free kids <12 |

| ST. CHARLES FALL FEST--HARTLAND (Fa 110) | | | |
|---|---|---|---|
| When? | Where? | Description and contact info | Admission |
| Early Sep., Fri., Sat., Sun., see website for hours | 313 Circle Drive, Hartland | Festival of rides, food, games, raffle, face-painting, scavenger hunt, and more. http://stcharlesfallfest.com/ | Free |

| NORTH PRAIRIE HARVESTFEST (Fa 111) | | | |
|---|---|---|---|
| When? | Where? | Description and contact info | Admission |
| Mid Sep., Fri. 5-11pm, Sat. 9am-11pm, Sun. 9am-5pm | Veterans Park, 13w N. Harrison St., North Prairie | Festival to celebrate autumn, vendors, pancake breakfast (not free), live music, carnival midway, parade, and more http://www.northprairie.net/ and https://www.facebook.com/North-Prairie-Harvest-Festival-452303668177157/ | Free |

| SHOREWOOD FARMERS MARKET (Fa 112) | | | |
|---|---|---|---|
| When? | Where? | Description and contact info | Admission |
| Sep.-early Nov., Sun. 9:30am-1pm | Lake Bluff Elementary, 1600 W. Bluff Blvd. | Fresh produce from Wisconsin farmers, baked goods, live entertainment, family events, arts, crafts. http://www.shorewoodfarmersmarket.com/ | Free |

| TRIMBORN FARM--GREENDALE (Fa 113) | | | |
|---|---|---|---|
| When? | Where? | Description and contact info | Admission |
| Sep.-Oct. 15, 10am-10pm; by appointment | 8881 W. Grange Ave., Greendale, WI | A guided tour of the only Milwaukee County park with a historic theme. Call 414-273-8288 to reserve a tour. http://www.milwaukeehistory.net/historic-sites-2/trimborn-farm/ | $5 for tour, kids < 6 free |

# Index

*Code: Yr = year round; Wi = Winter; Sp = Spring; Su = Summer; Fa = Fall*

## Outings outside of Milwaukee

Brookfield: BROOKFIELD FARMERS MARKET (Sp 42). (Su 140), (Fa 93); DOMINIC DAYS--BROOKFIELD (Su 185); WILSON CENTER GUITAR COMPETITION & FESTIVAL--BROOKFIELD (Su 211); NATIONAL NIGHT OUT--BROOKFIELD (Su 238).

Butler: BUTLER FARMERS MARKET (Su 221), (Fa 106); ST. AGNES PARISH FESTIVAL--BUTLER (Su 227).

Bayside: JULY 4TH PARADE--BAYSIDE (Su 24).

Big Bend: ST. JOSEPH FUN FEST—BIG BEND (Su 205); RUMBLE BY THE RIVER—BIG BEND (Su 207).

Brown Deer: SLEDDING—BROWN DEER (Wi 81); WELLNESS, BODY, MIND & SPIRIT EXPO—BROWN DEER (Sp 56) (Fa 99); BROWN DEER EAT & GREET ON THE STREET (Su 200);

Burlington: CHOCOLATE FEST--BURLINGTON (Sp 14).

Caledonia: ST. LOUIS PARISH FESTIVAL-CALEDONIA (Su 231).

Cedarburg: OZAUKEE COUNTY FAIR--CEDARBURG (Su 137); SUMMER SOUNDS IN CEDARBURG (Su 139); AGATE EXPO--CEDARBURG (Su 161); CEDARBURG PLEIN AIR PAINTING COMPETITION SHOW & SALE (Su 179); CEDARBURG WOMAN'S CLUB GARDEN WALK (Su 181); CEDARBURG STRAWBERRY FESTIVAL (Su 216); OKTOBERFEST--CEDARBURG (Fa 102); CEDARBURG WINE & HARVEST FESTIVAL (Fa 104).

Cudahy: SANTA IN THE PARK--CUDAHY (Wi 23); OUTDOOR ICE SKATING--CUDAHY (Wi 82); EASTER BUNNY AT PULASKI--CUDAHY (Sp 7); JULY 4TH CELEBRATION--CUDAHY (Su 21); SWEET APPLE-WOOD FESTIVAL--CUDAHY (Su 182); NATIONAL NIGHT OUT--CUDAHY (Su 240).

Delafield: DELAFIELD BLOCK PARTY (Su 180); LAKE COUNTRY ART FESTIVAL--DELAFIELD (Su 193); DELAFIELD FOOD AND MUSIC FESTIVAL (Su 196).

Eagle: KETTLE MORAINE DAYS--EAGLE (Su 162).

East Troy: CORN & BRAT ROAST—EAST TROY (Sp 13).

**Fox Point:** JULY 4TH PARADE—FOX POINT (Su 25).

**Franklin:** BINGO AT THE POLISH CENTER OF WISCONSIN-FRANKLIN (Yr67); LITTLE WONDERS: WOODLAND HOLIDAYS--FRANKLIN (Wi 29) (Sp 57), (Fa 97); ADULT OWL PROWL (Wi 68); SLEDDING--FRANKLIN (Wi 85); NATURE NAUTS: CRAZY OVER CRANES--FRANKLIN (Sp 41); FAMILY FROG FROLIC—FRANKLIN (Sp 49); MAPLE SUGAR DAYS--FRANKLIN (Sp 51); RE: CRAFT & RELIC--FRANKLIN (Sp 52), (Fa 109); CRAFT & RELIC SHOW--FRANKLIN (Sp 53); FRANKLIN CIVIC CELEBRATION (Su 20); CROATIANFEST--FRANKLIN (Su 156); LITTLE WONDERS--FRANKLIN (Su 198); NATIONAL NIGHT OUT--FRANKLIN (Su 224); SLOVAK-AMERICAN DAY--FRANKLIN (Su 233); XAVIERAN MISSION FESTIVAL--FRANKLIN (Su 235); HALLOWEEN HAUNTS--FRANKLIN (Fa 17).

**Franksville:** KRAUT MUSIC FEST--FRANKSVILLE (Su 141).

**Germantown:** ST. BONIFACE FALL FESTIVAL--GERMANTOWN (Fa 4).

**Glendale:** HANUKKAH STORYTIME WITH RABBI SHARI—BAYSHORE--GLENDALE (Wi 33); JULY 4TH CELEBRATION--GLENDALE (Su 27); NATIONAL NIGHT OUT--GLENDALE (Su 243); OKTOBERFEST--GLENDALE (Fa 101).

**Grafton:** HOT RODS-N-BLUES CAR SHOW--GRAFTON (Su 97); GRILLIN' IN GRAFTON (Su 186); GIRO D'GRAFTON (Su 199).

**Greendale:** JEREMIAH CURTIN HOUSE—GREENDALE (Yr66); OUTDOOR ICE SKATING-GREENDALE (Wi 92); TRIMBORN FARM--GREENDALE (Su 146) (Fa 113); GREENDALE LIONS CLUB VILLAGE DAYS (Su 167); GREENDALE VILLAGE DAYS (Su 209); OKTOBERFEST AT WHITNALL PARK BEER GARDEN--GREENDALE (Fa 103); HARVEST OF ARTS AND CRAFTS--GREENDALE (Fa 108).

**Greenfield:** DAN JANSEN FAMILY FEST--GREENFIELD (Sp 50); ST. JOHN THE EVANGELIST FAMILY FESTIVAL--GREENFIELD (Su 171); NATIONAL NIGHT OUT--GREENFIELD (Su 219).

**Hales Corners:** BOERNER HOLIDAY GIFT FAIR WITH SANTA—HALES CORNERS (Wi 28); OUTDOOR ICE SKATING— HALES CORNERS (Wi 90); SLEDDING—HALES CORNERS (Wi 95); EASTER DAY EVENT—HALES CORNERS (Sp 8); FAMILY EVENT: MAKE YOUR OWN FAIRY OR GNOME GARDEN—HALES CORNERS (Sp 43); JULY 4TH PARADE—HALES CORNERS (Su 29); CONCERT IN THE PARK—HALES CORNERS (Su 153); NATIONAL NIGHT OUT—HALES CORNERS (Su 220); ARTISTS IN THE GARDEN—HALES CORNERS (Su 223); ANNUAL GARDEN WALK—HALES CORNERS (Su 225); ST. MARY PARISH FESTIVAL—HALES CORNERS (Su 226); ANNUAL BONSAI EXHIBIT—HALES CORNERS (Fa 95).

**Hartford:** AMERICAN ACCENTS FESTIVAL OF FINE ARTS & CRAFTS--HARTFORD (Su 149).

**Hartland:** CANADIAN-PACIFIC HOLIDAY TRAIN STOP--HARTLAND (Wi 32); HARTLAND'S HOMETOWN CELEBRATION--HARTLAND (Su 166); ST. CHARLES FALL FEST--HARTLAND (Fa 110).

**Hubertus:** ART, CRAFTS & FARM MARKET SHOW--HUBERTUS (Su 151).

**Iola:** IOLA CAR SHOW & SWAP MEET (Su 232).

**Menomonee Falls:** MENOMONEE FALLS FARMERS MARKET (Sp 45) (Su 201) (Fa 90); ART IN THE PARK—MENOMONEE FALLS (Su 150); FALLS FEST—MENOMONEE FALLS (Su 170); OLD FALLS VILLAGE DAYS—MENOMONEE FALLS (Su 192); OLD FALLS VILLAGE CIVIL WAR ENCAMPMENT—MENOMONEE FALLS (Su 208).

**Mukwonago:** MUKWONAGO LIONS SUMMERFESTE (Su 3); CROATIAN DAY--MUKWONAGO (Su 194); ST. JAMES FAMILY FEST--MUKWONAGO (Su 229); NATIONAL NIGHT OUT--MUKWONAGO (Su 242).

**Muskego:** MUSKEGO COMMUNITY FESTIVAL--MUSKEGO (Su 169); NATIONAL NIGHT OUT--MUSKEGO (Su 237).

**North Prairie:** NORTH PRAIRIE HARVESTFEST (Fa 111).

**New Berlin:** LOW COST MOVIES: RIDGE THEATER-NEW BERLIN (Yr69); NEW BERLIN 4TH OF JULY FAMILY FESTIVAL (Su 28); ELIZABETH ANN SETON FUNFEST—NEW BERLIN (Su 164); HOLY APOSTLES FAMILY FESTIVAL—NEW BERLIN (Su 206); ANNUAL SCANDINAVIAN FESTIVAL—NEW BERLIN (Fa 89).

**Oak Creek:** LOW COST MOVIES: VALUE CINEMA-OAK CREEK (Yr68); EGYPTIAN COPTIC BAKE SALE—OAK CREEK (Wi 31); TASTE OF EGYPT—OAK CREEK (Su 165); OAK CREEK LIONSFEST (Fa 5);

**Oconomowoc:** OCONOMOWOC FESTIVAL OF THE ARTS (Su 215); NATIONAL NIGHT OUT--OCONOMOWOC (Su 241).

**Oshkosh:** EAA AIRVENTURE--OSHKOSH (Su 158).

**Pewaukee:** PEWAUKEE LAKE WATER SKI CLUB SHOW--PEWAUKEE (Sp 44) (Su 183); PEWAUKEE KIWANIS BEACH PARTY (Su 142); QUEEN OF APOSTLES FESTIVAL--PEWAUKEE (Su 178); TASTE OF LAKE COUNTRY--PEWAUKEE (Su 191).

**Plymouth:** IRISHMAN'S WALK--PLYMOUTH (Sp 3); GERMAN NIGHT--PLYMOUTH (Su 190); MILL STREET FESTIVAL--PLYMOUTH (Su 236).

**Port Washington:** COMMUNITY STREET FESTIVAL—PORT WASHINGTON (Sp 46).

Racine: MONUMENT SQUARE ART FESTIVAL--RACINE (Su 175); BOHEMIAN FEST--RACINE (Su 189); ST. RITA FAMILY FESTIVAL--RACINE (Su 195).

Sheboygan: MIDSUMMER FESTIVAL OF THE ARTS--SHEBOYGAN (Su 187).

St. Francis: ST. FRANCIS CHRISTMAS PARADE (Wi 34); BUDDY SQUIRREL ANNUAL EASTER OPEN HOUSE—ST. FRANCIS (Sp 9); JULY 4TH CELEBRATION—ST. FRANCIS (Su 22); ST. FRANCIS DAYS (Fa 6)

Shorewood: KILBOURNTOWN HOUSE—SHOREWOOD (Yr64); SHOREWOOD FARMERS MARKET (Su 157) (Fa 112); ST ROBERT FAIR--SHOREWOOD (Su 172);

South Milwaukee: JULY 4TH CELEBRATION—SOUTH MILWAUKEE (Su 19); NAVY BAND GREAT LAKES PERFORMANCE—SOUTH MILWAUKEE (Su 30); DIVINE MERCY FUNFEST—SOUTH MILWAUKEE (Su 203); SOUTH MILWAUKEE LIONSFEST (Su 204); NATIONAL NIGHT OUT—SOUTH MILWAUKEE (Su 239); ZOMBIE HOUSE AT THE MILL POND—SOUTH MILWAUKEE (Fa 18).

Sturtevant: CANADIAN-PACIFIC HOLIDAY TRAIN STOP--STURTEVANT (Wi 30).

Sussex: SUSSEX LIONS DAZE (Su 163).

Thiensville: THIENSVILLE-MEQUON LIONSFEST (Su 173).

Wales: DONNA LEXA MEMORIAL ART FAIR--WALES (Su 234).

Waterford: ST. THOMAS COUNTRY FAIR--WATERFORD (Su 174); WATERFORD BALLOON FESTIVAL (Su 230).

Waukesha: VALENTINE'S DAY TOBOGGANING--WAUKESHA (Wi 37); WAUKESHA JAMBOREE (Wi 80); ST. MARY'S FAMILY FUN FESTIVAL--WAUKESHA (Su 160); ST. JOHN NEUMANN FESTIVAL--WAUKESHA (Su 177); FIESTA WAUKESHA (Su 184); WAUKESHA COUNTY FAIR--WAUKESHA (Su 197); WAUKESHA OLD CAR CLUB SHOW & PICNIC (Su 210); SCOTTISH HIGHLAND GAMES—WISCONSIN--WAUKESHA (Fa 105).

Wauwatosa: LOWELL DAMON HOUSE—WAUWATOSA (Yr65); WAUWATOSA MERRY CHRISTMAS HOUSE--WAUWATOSA (Wi 24); CELTIC CHRISTMAS ARTS & CRAFTS SHOW--WAUWATOSA (Wi 25); CANADIAN-PACIFIC HOLIDAY TRAIN STOP--WAUWATOSA (Wi 26); OUTDOOR ICE SKATING--WAUWATOSA (Wi 93); SLEDDING--WAUWATOSA (Wi 98); GREECIAN FEST AT SAINTS CONSTANTINE AND HELEN CHURCH--WAUWATOSA (Su 143); FIREFLY ART FAIR--WAUWATOSA (Su 147); TOSA FARMERS MARKET (Su 152) (Fa 100); SCOTTISH HIGHLAND GAMES--WAUWATOSA (Su 217); NATIONAL NIGHT OUT--WAUWATOSA (Su 244); NATIONAL NIGHT OUT—ZOO WAUWATOSA (Su 245); TOSAFEST--WAUWATOSA (Fa 98).

**West Allis:** WEST ALLIS CHRISTMAS PARADE (Wi 35); ICE FISHING AND WINTER SPORT SHOW—WEST ALLIS (Wi 83); HMONG NEW YEAR—WEST ALLIS (Wi 86); WONDERFUL WORLD OF WEDDINGS—WEST ALLIS (Wi 87); MILWAUKEE BOAT SHOW—WEST ALLIS (Wi 88); GREAT LAKES PET EXPO—WEST ALLIS (Wi 89); OUTDOOR ICE SKATING—WEST ALLIS (Wi 91); WOMAN UP!—WEST ALLIS (Wi 94); MILWAUKEE/NARI SPRING IMPROVEMENT SHOW—WEST ALLIS (Wi 96); MILWAUKEE RV SHOW—WEST ALLIS (Wi 97); WEST ALLIS FARMERS MARKET (Sp 47) (Su 155) (Fa 92); IMMACULATE HEART OF MARY FESTIVAL—WEST ALLIS (Sp 48) IMMACULATE HEART OF MARY FESTIVAL—WEST ALLIS (Sp 48); MILWAUKEE JOURNAL SENTINEL SPORTS SHOW—WEST ALLIS (Sp 54); WINTER POWWOW—WEST ALLIS (Sp 55); WEDNESDAY NIGHT THUNDER—WEST ALLIS (Su 144); WEDNESDAY NIGHT LIVE—WEST ALLIS (Su 145); GREEK FEST—WEST ALLIS (Su 148); ST. RITA PARISH FESTIVAL—WEST ALLIS (Su 168); ST. ALOYSIUS FESTIVAL—WEST ALLIS (Su 176); WEST ALLIS ALA CARTE (Su 202); WISCONSIN STATE FAIR--$2 THURSDAY—WEST ALLIS (Su 213); WISCONSIN STATE FAIR—FAMILY FUN MONDAY—WEST ALLIS (Su 214); THURSDAY NIGHT THUNDER—WEST ALLIS (Su 222); ST. MATTHIAS FESTIVAL—WEST ALLIS (Su 228); HALLOWEEN AT GREENFIELD PARK—WEST ALLIS (Fa 16); HOLIDAY FOLK FAIR INTERNATIONAL--WEST ALLIS (Fa 88); HORSE EXPO—WEST ALLIS (Fa 91); MAKER FAIRE MILWAUKEE—WEST ALLIS (Fa 94); HARVEST FAIR—WEST ALLIS (Fa 107).

**West Bend:** MUSIC ON MAIN—WEST BEND (Su 138); WEST BEND GERMANFEST (Su 154; HOLY ANGELS FESTIVAL OF ANGELS—WEST BEND (Su 188); WASHINGTON COUNTY FAIR—WEST BEND (Su 212); RUMMAGE-A-RAMA—WEST BEND (Su 218) (Fa 96).

**Whitefish Bay:** GALLERY 505—WHITEFISH BAY (Yr63); COMMUNITY-WIDE HANUKKAH CELEBRATION—WHITEFISH BAY (Wi 27); JULY 4TH PARADE—WHITEFISH BAY (Su 26)

## Outings by category

**Block/school community events:** WEEKLY WALKS IN LINDSAY HEIGHTS (Yr20); ESCUELA VERDE'S COMMUNITY NIGHT (Sp 38); HISTORIC MITCHELL SUNFAIR (Su 78); BUCKS SUMMER BLOCK PARTY (Su 79); BRADY ST. FESTIVAL (Su 110); CENTER STREET DAYS (Su 121); LOCUST STREET FESTIVAL OF MUSIC AND ART (Su 124); COMMUNITY UNITY DAY BLOCK PARTY (Su 129); DELAFIELD BLOCK PARTY (Su 180); SAINTS PETER & PAUL BLOCK PARTY (Fa 23).

**Cars/motorcycles/trucks/RVs** (*e.g., races, exhibitions*): MILWAUKEE RV SHOW—WEST ALLIS (Wi 97); A.W.E.'S SUMMER TRUCK PROGRAM (Su 34); HOT RODS-N-BLUES CAR SHOW--GRAFTON (Su 97); WEDNESDAY NIGHT THUNDER—WEST ALLIS (Su 144); OLD FALLS VILLAGE DAYS—MENOMONEE FALLS (Su 192); RUMBLE BY THE RIVER—BIG BEND (Su 207); WAUKESHA OLD CAR CLUB SHOW & PICNIC (Su 210); THURSDAY NIGHT THUNDER—WEST ALLIS (Su 222); IOLA CAR SHOW & SWAP MEET (Su 232); GRANVILLE BID CAR, TRUCK, AND BIKE SPECTACULAR (Fa 82).

**Child-specific** (*young*): BETTY BRINN CHILDREN'S MUSEUM (Yr43); SATURDAY PRE-SCHOOL SERIES (Sp 21) (Wi 54) (Su 53) (Fa 48); WINTERFEST FOR AFTERNOON NAPPERS (Wi 74); CROSS COUNTRY SKIING FOR KIDS (Wi 77); HAPPY BIRTHDAY DR. SEUSS (Sp 33); LITTLE WONDERS--FRANKLIN (Sp 57) (Su 198) (Fa 97); SECRET GARDEN (Su 99); STORY TIME AT THE DOMES (Fa 86).

## Community pride/involvement: DOWNTOWN EMPLOYEE APPRECIATION WEEK (Su 55); NATIONAL NIGHT OUT—WEDGEWOOD PARK (Su 83); NATIONAL NIGHT OUT—NEAR WEST SIDE (Su 104); NATIONAL NIGHT OUT--SOUTH SIDE (Su 115); NATIONAL NIGHT OUT—NORTHWEST SIDE (Su 120); NATIONAL NIGHT OUT—NORTH SIDE (Su 122); WORLD REFUGEE DAY (Su 130); OLD FALLS VILLAGE DAYS—MENOMONEE FALLS (Su 192); WEST ALLIS ALA CARTE (Su 202); NATIONAL NIGHT OUT--GREENFIELD (Su 219); NATIONAL NIGHT OUT—HALES CORNERS (Su 220); NATIONAL NIGHT OUT--FRANKLIN (Su 224); NATIONAL NIGHT OUT--MUSKEGO (Su 237); NATIONAL NIGHT OUT--BROOKFIELD (Su 238); NATIONAL NIGHT OUT—SOUTH MILWAUKEE (Su 239); NATIONAL NIGHT OUT--CUDAHY (Su 240); NATIONAL NIGHT OUT--OCONOMOWOC (Su 241); NATIONAL NIGHT OUT--MUKWONAGO (Su 242); NATIONAL NIGHT OUT--GLENDALE (Su 243); NATIONAL NIGHT OUT--WAUWATOSA (Su 244); NATIONAL NIGHT OUT—ZOO WAUWATOSA (Su 245).

## Enrichment, general *(e.g., films, tours, lectures, history, architecture, museums, literature, poetry, gardens)*: OLD SOUTH SIDE SETTLEMENT MUSEUM (Yr2); SELF-GUIDED TOUR OF FOREST HOME CEMETERY (Yr2); MILLER-COORS TOUR (Yr3); CHUDNOW MUSEUM OF YESTERYEAR (Yr6); LOW COST MOVIES: DOWNER THEATER (Yr7); LOW COST MOVIES: ORIENTAL THEATER (Yr8); MILWAUKEE COUNTY HISTORICAL SOCIETY (Yr13); MOVIE TIME AT THE CHARLES ALLIS MUSEUM (Yr14); TOUR OF BEUHAH BRINTON HOUSE (Yr17); SELF-GUIDED TOUR OF VA GROUNDS (Yr18); MOVIES AT SOUTHGATE CINEMA (Yr19); JEWISH MUSEUM OF MILWAUKEE (Yr21); ARCHAEOLOGY LECTURES (Yr29; NORTHPOINT LIGHTHOUSE MUSEUM (Yr32); TOUR OF MUSEUM OF WISCONSIN EVANGELICAL LUTHERAN SYNOD (WELS) (Yr36); UNGUIDED TOUR OF BASILICA OF ST. JOSAPHAT (Yr39); GUIDED TOUR OF BASILICA OF ST. JOSAPHAT (Yr40); MITCHELL PARK DOMES (Yr44); MILWAUKEE PUBLIC MUSEUM (Yr45); FRENCH FILM SERIES (Yr58); MILWAUKEE FIRE MUSEUM (Yr60); KILBOURNTOWN HOUSE—SHOREWOOD (Yr64); LOWELL DAMON HOUSE—WAUWATOSA (Yr65); JEREMIAH CURTIN HOUSE—GREENDALE (Yr66); LOW COST MOVIES: VALUE CINEMA-OAK CREEK (Yr68); LOW COST MOVIES: RIDGE THEATER-NEW BERLIN (Yr69); FRENCH FILM FESTIVAL (Wi 40); ETHNIC FILMS (Wi ) (Wi 66); SKYWAUKEE WALKING TOUR (Wi 78) (Fa 87); GINGERBREAD LAND—HOLIDAY SHOW (Wi 79); GARDEN IMPRESSIONS SPRING FLORAL SHOW AT THE DOMES (Sp 18); OPEN HOUSE—ST. FRANCIS DE SALES SEMINARY (Sp 24); MILWAUKEE UNDERGROUND FILM FEST (Sp 25); STUDENT FILM AND VIDEO FESTIVAL (Sp 26); UWM'S LATIN AMERICAN FILM SERIES (Sp 28); PECK FLICKS (Su 33); WALKING TOUR—RIVER WALK (Su 35) (Fa 25); WALKING TOUR—HISTORIC THIRD WARD (Su 36) (Fa 27); WALKING TOUR—HISTORIC MILWAUKEE DOWNTOWN (Su 37) (Fa 24); WALKING TOUR—BRADY STREET (Su 65) (Fa 33; WALKING TOUR—NORTH POINT MANSIONS (Su 66); NATIONAL LIGHTHOUSE DAY (Su 69); WALKING TOUR—BAY VIEW (Su 75); POETRY IN THE PARK (Su 84); LAKEFRONT MOVIES (Su 88); SUMMER ON OLYMPUS: SUMMER FLORAL SHOW (Su 89); WALKING TOUR—BAY VIEW (Su 128) (Fa 34); TRIMBORN FARM--GREENDALE (Su 146) (Fa 113); CEDARBURG WOMAN'S CLUB GARDEN WALK (Su 181); OLD FALLS VILLAGE CIVIL WAR ENCAMPMENT—MENOMONEE FALLS (Su 208); ANNUAL GARDEN WALK—HALES CORNERS (Su 225); DOORS OPEN MILWAUKEE (Fa 22); MILWAUKEE SHORT FILM FESTIVAL (Fa 57); POETRY IN THE PARK (Fa 75); TOUR OF JONES ISLAND WATER RECLAMATION FACILITY (Fa 81); FALL FLORAL SHOW (Fa 84); ANNUAL BONSAI EXHIBIT—HALES CORNERS (Fa 95).

## Enrichment, arts (e.g., crafts, art, plays, décor, culinary): WALKER'S POINT CENTER FOR THE ARTS (Yr4); DEAN JENSEN GALLERY (Yr5); KERR GALLERY (Yr9); VILLA TERRACE DECORATIVE ARTS MUSEUM (Yr10); ORANGE GALLERY (Yr11); CHARLES ALLIS ART MUSEUM (Yr12); HAGGERTY MUSEUM OF ART (Yr16); GROHMANN MUSEUM (Yr22); ART BAR (Yr23); THE GREEN GALLERY (Yr24); ART 'N ODDITIES (Yr25); KATIE GINGRASS GALLERY (Yr26); GALLERY AT MILWAUKEE INSTITUTE OF ART & DESIGN (Yr33); MILWAUKEE ART MUSEUM (Yr42); MORNING GLORY GALLERY (Yr46); DAVID BARNETT ART GALLERY (Yr61); GALLERY 505—WHITEFISH BAY (Yr63); GALLERY NIGHT AND DAY (Wi 41) (Sp 19) (Su 41) (Fa 37); GUEST LECTURE SERIES ON THE ARTS (Wi 43); WEST SIDE ART WALK (Sp 16); GARDEN DISTRICT CRAFT FAIR (Sp

20); **GARDEN DISTRICT ART MARKET** (Su 57); **SHAKESPEARE IN THREE BRIDGES PARK** (Su 51); **TEMPORARY RESURFACING** (Su 77); **LAKEFRONT FESTIVAL OF THE ARTS** (Su 94); **WISCONSIN LUTHERAN ART & CRAFT FAIR** (Su 109); **MORNING GLORY FINE CRAFT FAIR** (Su 114); **BRONZEVILLE WEEK** (Su 119); **FIREFLY ART FAIR--WAUWATOSA** (Su 147); **AMERICAN ACCENTS FESTIVAL OF FINE ARTS & CRAFTS--HARTFORD** (Su 149); **ART IN THE PARK—MENOMONEE FALLS** (Su 150); **ART, CRAFTS & FARM MARKET SHOW--HUBERTUS** (Su 151); **MONUMENT SQUARE ART FESTIVAL--RACINE** (Su 175); **CEDARBURG PLEIN AIR PAINTING COMPETITION SHOW & SALE** (Su 179); **MIDSUMMER FESTIVAL OF THE ARTS--SHEBOYGAN** (Su 187); **HOLY ANGELS FESTIVAL OF ANGELS—WEST BEND** (Su 188); **LAKE COUNTRY ART FESTIVAL--DELAFIELD** (Su 193); **OCONOMOWOC FESTIVAL OF THE ARTS** (Su 21 **DONNA LEXA MEMORIAL ART FAIR--WALES** (Su 234) **DONNA LEXA MEMORIAL ART FAIR--WALES** (Su 234); **RIVERWEST ART WALK** (Fa 29); **THIRD WARD ART FESTIVAL** (Fa 32); **ANNUAL STARVING ARTISTS SALE** (Fa 35); **GRACE FINE ART & CRAFT FESTIVAL** (Fa 47); **GUEST LECTURE SERIES ON THE ARTS** (Fa 62); **HARVEST OF ARTS AND CRAFTS--GREENDALE** (Fa 108);

## Enrichment, concerts: MUSIC UNDER GLASS (Wi 72); CANTOS DE LAS AMERICAS (Sp 34); NAVY BAND GREAT LAKES PERFORMANCE—SOUTH MILWAUKEE (Su 30); KIDS FROM WISCONSIN (Su 32); CHILL ON THE HILL (Su 50); WEDNESDAYS AT THE SHELL IN WASHINGTON PARK (Su 54); BRONZEVILLE JAZZ IN THE HOOD (Su 58); AUGUST NIGHTS CONCERTS (Su 63); RIVER RHYTHMS (Su 70); MUSIC AND DANCE AT THE PECK (Su 82); MUSICAL MONDAYS (Su 93); WONDERFUL WEDNESDAYS (Su 95); RHYTHM & BLOOM CONCERT SERIES (Su 98); US AIR FORCE BAND OF MID-AMERICA CONCERT (Su 103); SUMMER EVENINGS OF MUSIC (Su 123); JAZZ IN THE PARK (Su 126); LIVE AT THE LAKE (Su 127); SKYLINE MUSIC SERIES (Su 131); AYRE IN THE SQUARE (Su 132); SUMMERFEST FOR FREE (Su 134); MUSIC ON MAIN—WEST BEND (Su 138); SUMMER SOUNDS IN CEDARBURG (Su 139); KRAUT MUSIC FEST--FRANKSVILLE (Su 141) KRAUT MUSIC FEST--FRANKSVILLE (Su 141); WEDNESDAY NIGHT LIVE—WEST ALLIS (Su 145); CONCERT IN THE PARK—HALES CORNERS (Su 153).

## Enrichment, ecology/nature: ECO ART WEDNESDAYS (Yr34); EARLY MORNING BIRDWALK (Yr35); EARLY MORNING BIRDWALK--WASHINGTON (Yr37); EARLY MORNING BIRDWALK--RIVERSIDE (Yr38); LITTLE NATURE MUSEUM (Yr47); WOOLY BEAR FEST (Wi 60); ADULT OWL PROWL (Wi 68); OWL PROWL FOR FAMILIES (Wi 76); MAPLE SUGARING AT RIVERSIDE (Sp 20); WARBLER WALKS IN LAKE PARK (Sp 36); NATURE NAUTS: CRAZY OVER CRANES--FRANKLIN (Sp 41); FAMILY EVENT: MAKE YOUR OWN FAIRY OR GNOME GARDEN—HALES CORNERS (Sp 43); DAIRY FARM FUN DAY (Su 39); ENCHANTED FOREST (Fa 56).

## Enrichment, ethnic and diverse populations: MILWAUKEE ASIAN MARKET (Yr30); FRENCH FILM SERIES (Yr58); WALK THROUGH MILWAUKEE'S LATINO HISTORY (Yr59); WALK THROUGH OLD BRONZEVILLE (Yr62); BINGO AT THE POLISH CENTER OF WISCONSIN-FRANKLIN (Yr67); EGYPTIAN COPTIC BAKE SALE—OAK CREEK (Wi 31); KWANZAA AT BODY & SOUL (Wi 6); KWANZAA—BHM (Wi 7); CELTIC CHRISTMAS ARTS & CRAFTS SHOW--WAUWATOSA (Wi 25); COMMUNITY-WIDE HANUKKAH CELEBRATION—WHITEFISH BAY (Wi 27); HANUKKAH STORYTIME WITH RABBI SHARI—BAYSHORE--GLENDALE (Wi 33); MARTIN LUTHER KING CELEBRATION (Wi 38); DR. MARTIN LUTHER KING JR. CELEBRATION (Wi 39); FRENCH FILM FESTIVAL (Wi 40); ETHNIC FILMS (Wi ) (Wi 66); HMONG NEW YEAR—WEST ALLIS (Wi 86); WOMAN UP!—WEST ALLIS (Wi 94); ST. PATRICK'S DAY PARADE (Sp 1); POST ST. PATRICK'S DAY PARADE PARTY (Sp 2); IRISHMAN'S WALK--PLYMOUTH (Sp 3); BAVARIAN MAIFEST (Sp 15); UWM'S LATIN AMERICAN FILM SERIES (Sp 28); CZECH/SLOVAK GYMNASTICS EXHIBITION (Sp 31); CANTOS DE LAS AMERICAS (Sp 34); MILWAUKEE MUSLIM FILM FESTIVAL (Sp 39); IMMACULATE HEART OF MARY FESTIVAL—WEST ALLIS (Sp 48); WINTER POWWOW—WEST ALLIS (Sp 55); JUNETEENTH DAY (Su 1); PICNIC: AFRICANS IN MILWAUKEE (Su 38); ASIA FEST (Su 42); BRONZEVILLE JAZZ IN THE HOOD (Su 58) BRONZEVILLE JAZZ IN THE HOOD (Su 58); GAY PRIDE PARADE (Su 64); TASTE OF ISLANDS, JAMAICA (Su 73); POLISH FEST FRIDAY PROMOTION (Su 85); POLISH FEST

SATURDAY PROMOTION (Su 86); ARMENIAN FEST (Su 91; FESTA ITALIANA (Su 100); IRISH FEST FRIDAY PROMOTION (Su 101); GERMAN FEST FRIDAY PROMOTION (Su 102); MILWAUKEE DRAGON BOAT FESTIVAL (Su 107); INDIAFEST (Su 108); FREE MEXICAN FIESTA (Su 112); BASTILLE DAYS (Su 118); BRONZEVILLE WEEK (Su 119); PUERTO RICAN FEST (Su 133); KASHUBIAN PICNIC (Su 136); GREECIAN FEST AT SAINTS CONSTANTINE AND HELEN CHURCH--WAUWATOSA (Su 143); GREEK FEST—WEST ALLIS (Su 148); WEST BEND GERMANFEST (Su 154); CROATIANFEST--FRANKLIN (Su 156); TASTE OF EGYPT—OAK CREEK (Su 165); FIESTA WAUKESHA (Su 184); BOHEMIAN FEST--RACINE (Su 189); GERMAN NIGHT--PLYMOUTH (Su 190); CROATIAN DAY--MUKWONAGO (Su 194); SCOTTISH HIGHLAND GAMES--WAUWATOSA (Su 217); SLOVAK-AMERICAN DAY--FRANKLIN (Su 233); DIA DE LOS MUERTOS (Fa 10); LATINO FAMILY EXPO & FESTIVAL (Fa 14); HUNTING MOON POW WOW (Fa 28); OKTOBERFEST AT TOSA FARMERS MARKET (Fa 30); OKTOBERFEST AT PERE MARQUETTE (Fa 53); MILWAUKEE LGBT FILM FESTIVAL (Fa 59); SILVER CITY INTERNATIONAL FOOD AND ART WALK (Fa 60); INDIAN SUMMER (Fa 64); UMOS MEXICAN INDEPENDENCE DAY PARADE (Fa 66); UMOS MEXICAN INDEPENCE DAY FESTIVAL (Fa 67); OKTOBERFEST ARTISAN FAIR (Fa 85); HOLIDAY FOLK FAIR INTERNATIONAL--WEST ALLIS (Fa 88); ANNUAL SCANDINAVIAN FESTIVAL—NEW BERLIN (Fa 89); OKTOBERFEST--GLENDALE (Fa 101); OKTOBERFEST--CEDARBURG (Fa 102); OKTOBERFEST AT WHITNALL PARK BEER GARDEN--GREENDALE (Fa 103); SCOTTISH HIGHLAND GAMES—WISCONSIN--WAUKESHA (Fa 105);

# Enrichment, science (e.g., astronomy, biology, physics, health, alternative health):
UWM SCIENCE BAG (Yr41); GLORIOUS GALAXIES (Wi 63); CUPID'S CONSTELLATIONS (Wi 64); WELLNESS, BODY, MIND & SPIRIT EXPO—BROWN DEER (Sp 56) (Fa 99); URBAN STARGAZING (Su 87); STARS & S'MORES (Su 105); TIE-DYING SHIRTS (Su 106); ANNUAL HEALTH FEST (Fa 50).

# Fairs/festivals (e.g. rides, picnic, vendors, food):
CORN & BRAT ROAST—EAST TROY (Sp 13); CHOCOLATE FEST--BURLINGTON (Sp 14); FAMILY KITE FESTIVAL (Sp 37); COMMUNITY STREET FESTIVAL—PORT WASHINGTON (Sp 46); IMMACULATE HEART OF MARY FESTIVAL—WEST ALLIS (Sp 48); FAMILY FROG FROLIC—FRANKLIN (Sp 49); DAN JANSEN FAMILY FEST--GREENFIELD (Sp 50); MAPLE SUGAR DAYS--FRANKLIN (Sp 51); MUKWONAGO LIONS SUMMERFESTE (Su 3); ST. BERNADETTE PARISH FESTIVAL (Su 44); BASILICA PARISH PICNIC (Su 45); ST. PAUL PARISH FESTIVAL (Su 46); ST. ROMAN'S FESTIVAL (Su 62); ST. ADALBERT PARISH FESTIVAL (Su 71); ST. ROMAN'S ANNUAL FESTIVAL (Su 90); ST. MATTHIAS PARISH FESTIVAL (Su 111); SUMMER SOULSTICE MUSIC FEST (Su 113); SUMMERFEST FOR FREE (Su 134); SOUTH SHORE FROLICS (Su 135); OZAUKEE COUNTY FAIR--CEDARBURG (Su 137); KRAUT MUSIC FEST--FRANKSVILLE (Su 141); PEWAUKEE KIWANIS BEACH PARTY (Su 142); EAA AIRVENTURE--OSHKOSH (Su 158); ST. MARY'S FAMILY FUN FESTIVAL--WAUKESHA (Su 160); KETTLE MORAINE DAYS--EAGLE (Su 162); SUSSEX LIONS DAZE (Su 163); ELIZABETH ANN SETON FUNFEST—NEW BERLIN (Su 164); HARTLAND'S HOMETOWN CELEBRATION--HARTLAND (Su 166); GREENDALE LIONS CLUB VILLAGE DAYS (Su 167); ST. RITA PARISH FESTIVAL—WEST ALLIS (Su 168); MUSKEGO COMMUNITY FESTIVAL--MUSKEGO (Su 169); FALLS FEST—MENOMONEE FALLS (Su 170); ST. JOHN THE EVANGELIST FAMILY FESTIVAL--GREENFIELD (Su 171); ST ROBERT FAIR--SHOREWOOD (Su 172); THIENSVILLE-MEQUON LIONSFEST (Su 173); ST. THOMAS COUNTRY FAIR--WATERFORD (Su 174); ST. ALOYSIUS FESTIVAL—WEST ALLIS (Su 176); ST. JOHN NEUMANN FESTIVAL--WAUKESHA (Su 177); QUEEN OF APOSTLES FESTIVAL--PEWAUKEE (Su 178); SWEET APPLE-WOOD FESTIVAL--CUDAHY (Su 182); DOMINIC DAYS--BROOKFIELD (Su 185); GRILLIN' IN GRAFTON (Su 186); HOLY ANGELS FESTIVAL OF ANGELS—WEST BEND (Su 188); TASTE OF LAKE COUNTRY--PEWAUKEE (Su 191); OLD FALLS VILLAGE DAYS—MENOMONEE FALLS (Su 192); ST. RITA FAMILY FESTIVAL--RACINE (Su 195); DELAFIELD FOOD AND MUSIC FESTIVAL (Su 196); WAUKESHA COUNTY FAIR--WAUKESHA (Su 197); BROWN DEER EAT & GREET ON THE STREET (Su 200); DIVINE MERCY FUNFEST—SOUTH MILWAUKEE (Su 203); SOUTH MILWAUKEE LIONSFEST (Su 204); ST. JOSEPH FUN FEST—BIG BEND (Su 205); HOLY APOSTLES FAMILY FESTIVAL—NEW BERLIN (Su 206); GREENDALE VILLAGE DAYS (Su 209); WILSON CENTER GUITAR COMPETITION & FESTIVAL--BROOKFIELD (Su 211); WASHINGTON COUNTY FAIR—WEST BEND (Su 212); WISCONSIN

STATE FAIR--$2 THURSDAY—WEST ALLIS (Su 213); WISCONSIN STATE FAIR—FAMILY FUN MONDAY—WEST ALLIS (Su 214); CEDARBURG STRAWBERRY FESTIVAL (Su 216); ST. MARY PARISH FESTIVAL—HALES CORNERS (Su 226); ST. AGNES PARISH FESTIVAL--BUTLER (Su 227); ST. MATTHIAS FESTIVAL—WEST ALLIS (Su 228); ST. JAMES FAMILY FEST--MUKWONAGO (Su 229); WATERFORD BALLOON FESTIVAL (Su 230); ST. LOUIS PARISH FESTIVAL-CALEDONIA (Su 231) ST. LOUIS PARISH FESTIVAL-CALEDONIA (Su 231); XAVIERAN MISSION FESTIVAL--FRANKLIN (Su 235); MILL STREET FEVSTIAL—PLYMOUTH (Su 236); ST. BONIFACE FALL FESTIVAL--GERMANTOWN (Fa 4); OAK CREEK LIONSFEST (Fa 5); ST. FRANCIS DAYS (Fa 6); ST. GREGORY THE GREAT FESTIVAL (Fa 39); MILWAUKEE COFFEE FESTIVAL PRESENTED BY PENDULUM COFFEE (Fa 40); GREGORY THE GREAT PARISH FESTIVAL (Fa 55); BAY VIEW BASH (Fa 58); HARVEST FEST AT THE LIBRARY (Fa 78); CENTER STREET PARK FALL FEST (Fa 79); TOSAFEST--WAUWATOSA (Fa 98); CEDARBURG WINE & HARVEST FESTIVAL (Fa 104); HARVEST FAIR—WEST ALLIS (Fa 107); ST. CHARLES FALL FEST--HARTLAND (Fa 110); NORTH PRAIRIE HARVESTFEST (Fa 111).

## Games/contests (*e.g. cards, billiards, magic, board games*): MONTHLY FAMILY MAGIC SHOW (Yr15); MERRILL PARK PLAYFIELD/COMMUNITY CENTER (Yr50); BILLIARDS—BAY VIEW (Yr56); CARD PLAYING—BAY VIEW (Yr 57); BINGO AT THE POLISH CENTER OF WISCONSIN-FRANKLIN (Yr67).

## Pets/animals (*zoos, pet outings*): DOG PHOTOS WITH SANTA (Wi 17); ADULT OWL PROWL (Wi 68); FAMILY FREE DAY AT THE ZOO (Wi 73) (Sp 35) (Fa 77); OWL PROWL FOR FAMILIES (Wi 76); GREAT LAKES PET EXPO—WEST ALLIS (Wi 89); NATURE NAUTS: CRAZY OVER CRANES--FRANKLIN (Sp 41); BRADY STREET PET PARADE (Fa 71); FROMM PET FEST (Fa 80); HORSE EXPO—WEST ALLIS (Fa 91).

## Special markets (*e.g., farmers, antiques, rummage; specialty products*):
MILWAUKEE COUNTY WINTER FARMERS MARKET (Wi 44) (Sp 17) (Fa 31); WONDERFUL WORLD OF WEDDINGS—WEST ALLIS (Wi 87); MILWAUKEE/NARI SPRING IMPROVEMENT SHOW—WEST ALLIS (Wi 96); FONDY FARMERS MARKET (Sp 29) (Su 43) (Fa 63); BROOKFIELD FARMERS MARKET (Sp 42) (Su 140) (Fa 93); MENOMONEE FALLS FARMERS MARKET (Sp 45) (Su 201) (Fa 90); WEST ALLIS FARMERS MARKET (Sp 47) (Su 155) (Fa 92); CRAFT & RELIC--FRANKLIN (Sp 52) (Fa 109); RIVERWEST GARDENERS MARKET (Su 40) (Fa 36); SOUTH SHORE FARMERS MARKET (Su 48) (Fa 41); JACKSON PARK FARMERS MARKET (Su 56) (Fa 44); WALKER'S SQUARE FARMERS MARKET (Su 59) (Fa 45); WESTOWN FARMERS MARKET (Su 60) (Fa 38); CATHEDRAL SQUARE MARKET (Su 67) (Fa 42); HARAMBE COMMUNITY MARKET (Su 68) (Fa 43); GARDEN DISTRICT FARMERS MARKET (Su 80) (Fa 61); FONDY'S FARMERS MARKET—SCHLITZ PARK (Su 96) (Fa 46); TOSA FARMERS MARKET (Su 152) (Fa 100); SHOREWOOD FARMERS MARKET (Su 157) (Fa 112); AGATE EXPO--CEDARBURG (Su 161); RUMMAGE-A-RAMA—WEST BEND (Su 218); BUTLER FARMERS MARKET (Su 221) (Fa 106); ANNUAL STARVING ARTISTS SALE (Fa 35); MAKER FAIRE MILWAUKEE—WEST ALLIS (Fa 94); RUMMAGE-A-RAMA—WEST BEND (Fa 96).

## Sports (*e.g., races, cycling, skating, swimming, hunting, fishing, boating, spectator, sledding, skiing*): OPEN SWIM—PULASKI (Yr27); OPEN SWIM—NOYES (Yr28); HANK AARON TRAIL (Yr31); FREE FAMILY SWIM—WASHINGTON HS (Yr48); FREE FAMILY SWIM—GAENSLEN HS (Yr49); MERRILL PARK PLAYFIELD/COMMUNITY CENTER (Yr50); FREE FAMILY SWIM—NORTH DIVISION (Yr51); FREE FAMILY SWIM—SOUTH DIVISION (Yr52); FREE FAMILY SWIM—MORSE-MARSHALL (Yr53); FREE FAMILY SWIM—RIVERSIDE (Yr54); BASKETBALL—BAY VIEW (Yr55); BILLIARDS—BAY VIEW (Yr56); SLEDDING--PULASKI (Wi 42); SLEDDING--WILSON (Wi 45); SLEDDING--MCGOVERN (Wi 46) SLEDDING--MCGOVERN (Wi 46); SLEDDING--MCCARTY (Wi 47); ROLLER SKATING NIGHTS (Wi 48) (Su 52) (Fa 51); OUTDOOR ICE SKATING—DOWNTOWN (Wi 49); OUTDOOR ICE SKATING--RAINBOW (Wi 50); OUTDOOR ICE SKATING—BAY VIEW (Wi 51); OUTDOOR ICE SKATING—LAKE PARK (Wi 5); OUTDOOR ICE SKATING—LAFOLLETTE RINK (Wi 53);

SLEDDING--LAFOLLETTE (Wi 55); **SLEDDING--GREEN** (Wi 56); **SLEDDING--COLUMBUS** (Wi 57); **SLEDDING--HUMBOLDT** (Wi 58); **MARQUETTE GOLDEN EAGLES GAMES** (Wi 59) (Fa 76); **MARQUETTE WOMEN'S BASKETBALL** (Wi 61) (Fa 72); **MILWAUKEE BUCKS GAMES** (Wi 62) (Sp 32); (Fa 74); **WINTER SPORTS** (Wi 65); **WATERSTONE BANK ICE RINK** (Wi 69); **PUBLIC ICE SKATING AT THE PETTIT** (Wi 70); **RUN/WALK TRACK AT THE PETTIT** (Wi 71); **SLEDDING THE SLOPES OF MENOMONEE VALLEY** (Wi 75); **WAUKESHA JAMBOREE** (Wi 80); **SLEDDING—BROWN DEER** (Wi 81); **OUTDOOR ICE SKATING--CUDAHY** (Wi 82); **ICE FISHING & WINTER SPORTS SHOW—WEST ALLIS** (Wi 84); **SLEDDING--FRANKLIN** (Wi 85); **MILWAUKEE BOAT SHOW—WEST ALLIS** (Wi 88); **OUTDOOR ICE SKATING— HALES CORNERS** (Wi 90); **OUTDOOR ICE SKATING—WEST ALLIS** (Wi 91); **OUTDOOR ICE SKATING-GREENDALE** (Wi 92); **OUTDOOR ICE SKATING--WAUWATOSA** (Wi 93); **SLEDDING—HALES CORNERS** (Wi 95); **SLEDDING--WAUWATOSA** (Wi 98); **OPEN ROCK CLIMBING** (Sp 22) (Su 76);; **RENT A BIKE AT VETERANS PARK** (Sp 23); **FAMILY HIKE** (Sp 27); **CZECH/SLOVAK GYMNASTICS EXHIBITION** (Sp 31); **ROOT RIVER HIKE & BIKE** (Sp 40); **PEWAUKEE LAKE WATER SKI CLUB SHOW--PEWAUKEE** (Sp 44); **MILWAUKEE JOURNAL SENTINEL SPORTS SHOW—WEST ALLIS** (Sp 54); **RENT A BIKE AT VETERANS PARK** (Su 31) (Fa 65); **PELICAN GROVE SWIM** (Su 47); **DOWNER CLASSIC BIKE RACE** (Su 61); **FRIENDS OF HANK AARON STATE TRAIL 5K RUN/WALK** (Su 72); **FREE FISHING** (Su 74); **FELIX MANTILLA LITTLE LEAGUE GAMES** (Su 92); **PADDLE BOAT RENTALS** (Su 116) (Fa 68); **SAIL BOAT RENTALS** (Su 117) (Fa 69); **EAA AIRVENTURE--OSHKOSH** (Su 158); **PEWAUKEE LAKE WATER SKI CLUB SHOW--PEWAUKEE** (Su 183); **GIRO D'GRAFTON** (Su 199); **MILWAUKEE RUNNING FESTIVAL** (Fa 49); **FALL FAMILY PADDLE** (Fa 52); **FAMILY HIKE** (Fa 54).

## Senior-focused: **OASIS CENTER FOR OLDER ADULTS** (Yr27a); **BINGO AT THE POLISH CENTER OF WISCONSIN-FRANKLIN** (Yr67); **SENIORFEST** (Su 49).

**Do you have an event you'd like to submit for the 2019/2020 edition?**

Ask yourself the following questions:

1. Is this a recurring event at regular intervals (at least once annually)?
2. Is the price $10 or under for standard adult admission (regardless of residency, membership, etc.)?
3. Do you have contact information on this event (ideally a website)?

If "yes" to all three questions you may submit your event, with date, hours, address, description (<20 words), contact info, and admission price[s] to JFLanthropologist@sbcglobal.net.


**Do you have a change to an event you'd like to submit for the 2019/2020 edition?**

Do you have a correction to a listed event?
Has the event been discontinued?

Please submit the change to JFLanthropologist@sbcglobal.net. Please provide the number of the event and the title.